Beyond Tomorrow

J. Neville Ward

BEYOND TOMORROW

London
EPWORTH PRESS

Enquiries should be addressed to
The Methodist Publishing House
Wellington Road
Wimbledon
London SW19 8EU

7162 0362 6

Typeset by Gloucester Typesetting Services
and printed in Great Britain by
Richard Clay Ltd (The Chaucer Press)
Bungay, Suffolk

To Marsaili and Suzanne

ACKNOWLEDGMENTS

The author and publishers are indebted to the following for permission to use copyright material:

Sheldon Press for an extract from *The Wisdom of the Desert* by Thomas Merton;

Faber and Faber Ltd for a quotation from *The Collected Poems of Edwin Muir*;

David Higham Associates and William Heinemann for an extract from *The Chinese Love Pavilion* by Paul Scott.

CONTENTS

PREFACE

THESE CHAPTERS ARE an expansion of a series of public lectures I was invited to give in 1979 by the London branch of the William Temple Association. I am grateful to the Association at Liddon House and to the clergy of Grosvenor Chapel for the opportunity to consider with them these thoughts on the Lord's Prayer in the life of today.

The text I have used is that in Chapter 6 of St Matthew's Gospel in the Revised Standard Version.

66 Mount Road   NEVILLE WARD
Canterbury
1981

Our Father who art in heaven

THE LORD'S PRAYER must have come from Jesus' inner world, where he was truly himself, an insecure, loving man, prepared to take the risk of loving. These were the thoughts about life he had spent most time with; he had often taken counsel from them, he had survived on them when there was nothing else.

I believe this because I believe that he was not a patronizing person. So, when his friends asked to be helped to pray, he would not have given them any thoughts he had grown out of, as though he saw them as beginners, able to absorb only the first lesson. He would have given them what still counted with him, now steadied him, and took him straight to the truth of every situation.

He was also a man of experience. He had had some contact with life's tremendous interest, its pain, its way of leaving you guessing when you want the facts, so he would not be vapid. Their request went to his heart, and he answered it from his heart.

When, however, he told them to begin their prayers by calling God 'Father', he was not giving them a new idea. They were used to this way of approaching God. Indeed, many religions and world-views before and since Jesus' troubled time have thought of life as to be referred ultimately to a kind of fatherliness.

The rest of the prayer would not have surprised them either. Its words and ideas had all been in the minds of their countrymen for centuries. Jesus seemed to think them good enough.

The new thing, because there was indeed something new, was the remarkable warmth and affection with which Jesus apparently said and used the word 'Father'. And it could be said that the directness and brevity of the prayer he gave them was, if not exactly new, then certainly unusual. It is marvellously free from pietistic solemnity and verbal pretentiousness. It has the style of a man who never said more or less than he believed. That is part of what it means to have faith as Jesus had it.

When, in my adolescence, I first began trying to make up my mind about the world then opening itself up to me in the unmanageable rush of experience it is at that time, it was its beauty that shook me most. And when, more or less at the same time, I began my amateur attempt at understanding the Christian tradition into which I had been born, it was certainly not in any critical or dissatisfied mood. I had already found life good when I began thinking about God and what that famous word might mean. So, for me in those early days, there was no intellectual strain in calling God 'Father'.

As the years went through my fingers, like so many dropped catches, I found life making a very different impression on me. I look back now in sheer amazement at that young self who, in some distress or other, had only to hear a Mozart piano concerto for life to come right side up again. I did not immediately, or even quickly, notice this change of impression that life was secretly making, like the first deceits in a love affair. Eventually, however, in one example after another, a darker part of the truth became clear. As well as the music of Mozart, there are depths of pain and question and resentment in life that require a fair amount to be added to this one word 'Father' if Jesus is to remain credible.

That aspect of life has become increasingly clear to me, so that now after years of trying to understand Christianity I really have to struggle to save the word 'Father' for intelligible use. I do it, in part, by considering it an ultimate word, a word dealing with ultimate things. That is to say, it can be used only in faith and amazement initially.

The spiritual life is a matter of living and thinking in that unproven trust, beginning to find the word 'Father' less surprising, and gradually coming to think that it probably will indeed carry the day, that ultimately, in the eschatological beyond, it will be seen to be the one and only word to fit the universal meaning.

That kind of faith becomes both more precarious and more tenacious with every month one lives.

It is not the usual forms of pain that shock me most. I find them as disturbing as others do, but it seems to me that there are thoughts and attitudes within reach of most people that do help to lessen the outrageous character we initially may want to ascribe to such pain when we meet it.

What I have found increasingly unbearable relates to the very structure of creation, the vital process itself.

It cannot be denied that that process is in part a matter of one form of life pursuing, destroying and consuming some other form, which, whatever it is, represents a system of feeling and urgency, intricate, sensitive, often exquisite, always interesting to the point of fascination. That is an aspect of nature that I find quite revolting.

Two of the most beautiful lines in the prayers of the Bible are, 'The eyes of all wait upon thee, O Lord; and thou givest them their meat in due season.' Hidden in those lines there is the objectionable mystery of the predator and the prey, there is dread, there is a whole world of living things seeking what refuge there insufficiently is, there is the terrified scuffle in the forest.

I understand that Darwin said that to think of the suffering of the lower animals throughout time was more than he could bear. It endears the man to me and it makes me wonder whether there are any thoughts that God cannot bear. The pattern of the pursuing and the pursued, the caught, the torn, the devoured, is so general (and is by no means absent from the human world) that it seems dishonest not to notice it, not to admit the difficulty we would find in trying to fit its sombre detail explicitly into the *Te Deum*.

The cost of certain forms of knowledge is another mystery.

The price in millions of deaths that mankind is having to pay to learn how to create a stable structure of international peace seems to me quite unjustifiable. So does the automatism of history; I mean, that so little can be done about it. The accumulated weight of the past seems to leave too small a margin of freedom for each generation to improve things much. To that source I refer also the uneven development of civilization that leaves poverty and misery in one half of the world and deposits more material wealth and technical knowledge than it knows how to handle in the other half. And I see with dismay that how to right such imbalance defeats the wit of man, except when viewed in the longest of long terms.

There are, however, other reports on human experience which throw complicating lights into these shadows. It is a fact that generally speaking people who deeply believe in God rarely find their belief in him shaken by suffering; and indeed I believe this to be one of the principal marks of true faith.

The goodness of life is not evidence for our belief in the goodness of God, nor is the evil of life evidence for some case against him or for abandoning belief in him. Faith is *a way of interpreting* both the goodness and the evil of life. It can be argued that it is only in the presence of evil that faith most clearly looks like this and reveals itself as truly faith and not knowledge. For registering the aesthetic, faith may help and enhance, but it is not strictly necessary. The beautiful, except in some highly sophisticated forms of art, is obvious and just waits to be loved. To say the 'Our Father' is to say a prayer of 'unknowing', a prayer of faith; but we are able to see this much more clearly in our spells of personal darkness than we can in those periods when life is a joyful and amusing thing.

It is a commonplace that people's tolerance of suffering varies astonishingly. Love has much to do with this, because all the world over it is noticed that love can make suffering look very small. People who know, or have known, deep love are practically certain to say that whatever pain life has brought them (even the death of the beloved or the crumbling of the love) has not been as powerful in meaning as that love. They would not trade that love for a life without that pain.

It may be that everyone dimly sees that, when lit by the light of love, pain becomes bearable and even intelligible. In one of Tennessee Williams' plays a character argues that the greatest of all differences in this world is not between rich and poor, or even good and evil, but between those who have loved and those who have only watched it with envy.

I have come to believe, too, that there is some positive relation between outrageous evil and compassion.

If the evil and suffering of the world were logical throughout and it could be clearly shown that they and their causes make a sublimely reasonable pattern, that mistaken or wrong acts are the cause of all the varieties of unhappiness, and justly so, I do not think that compassion would thrive among us. We would find ourselves in a much bleaker world than this, a world in which all human beings dreadfully got their deserts.

As it is, being a realm in which sufferings repeatedly go beyond deserts, are often unjustifiable by any reasoning and are sometimes outrageous, human life is a tragic thing. As such, according to a famous classical principle, it repeatedly draws from human beings a redemptive pity and fear that a world of happiness would never be able even to imagine, never mind stimulate.

There is a poem by Edwin Muir in which he compares our imperfect world with the joyful perfection of the garden of Eden, and much to Eden's disadvantage. His view is that the harvest gathered from what he calls our disordered 'fields of charity and sin' could never grow in a perfect world:

> . . . famished field and blackened tree
> Bear flowers in Eden never known.
> Blossoms of grief and charity
> Bloom in these darkened fields alone.
> What had Eden ever to say
> Of hope and faith and pity and love
> Until was buried all its day
> And memory found its treasure trove?
> Strange blessings never in Paradise
> Fall from these beclouded skies.[1]

It has always seemed to me unwise to look to Jesus for help in the details of our twentieth-century agruments about religion. The faith of Jesus is not that of a man who has shared our complicated effort to think out a theology of prayer that takes account of the scientific world-view and its logical procedures.

His mind seems to have worked within the certainty that God's power, his involvement in the life of the world, and his desire to help us find our way to him, are all unlimited, and that he is to be trusted in the worst and the best that we encounter. Naturally, then, he turned to him in prayer.

At the same time, God is the tremendous mystery we cannot fathom, often seeming to hide his face though unexpectedly returning, always the one in whose will is our peace but never one into whose presence we can come with claims and presumptions.

This combination of infinite love and infinite mystery may put too much strain on struggling human minds, so that they cannot hold together two such vastnesses without splitting. The Jesus of the gospels, however, seems to me to be living day and night in that tension; and from that comes our sense of his being absolutely alive.

This is why, when Christian worship dies or is dead, it is generally because in one way or another it is expressing some evasion or rejection of the mystery and, accordingly, some claim on the love or presumption about it. The worshippers themselves may not realize this, but they know there is something wrong, they have an unpleasant sense of unreality and want to clear out of it into a more honourable mental atmosphere.

Living on the Christian assumptions means accepting the tensions involved, between God's love and the world's evil, between our faith that God desires to help us and the limitations he has evidently set for that help. It will always be hard to fit together our prayers and God's providence. These paradoxes and contradictions are like parallel lines that pursue an obstinately irreconcileable course in time but meet at infinity. God is the unity, the one, in whom all opposites are reconciled and, being reconciled, are themselves transformed into the unimaginable substance of the love that is his eternal kingdom.

It would be a mistake to understand this idea in purely chronological terms, as though by 'infinity' is meant simply 'that one far-off divine event to which the whole creation moves'. There are anticipations in which it all comes forward.

There are certain experiences in which hints of this ultimate reconciliation seem to be given here and now in our life in time. These experiences are accessible to everyone, however ignorant, sensual, despairing, since moments of openness and humility come to everyone. The mind gropes forward in its effort to understand itself and what it experiences, but at any moment (apparently not as a result of any kind of cleverness but of spiritual openness, itself usually an undeserved gift) the heavens can be rent and God descend to make your unsatisfactory heart his home.

The kind of life he has given us certainly has unnerving shifts of happiness and sadness, but it also has this extraordinary power of unexpectedly becoming exalted and mysterious, as though someone has suddenly turned on a brilliant and revealing light in a world that has always been half in shadow, making it a radiance and a home. I believe that something like that is what the gospels mean by a 'miracle', and it is a thousand miles away from the conventional and useless view of a miracle as an event that contravenes the laws of nature.

To most people, however, miracles are few and far between. You can direct your thoughts to a single ordinary life, or over centuries and nations, and you will find the same human mixture – intense happiness at times, often feelings of content and safety, and depths of pain underneath; sometimes a surface of great wretchedness and profound joy underneath; and everywhere people who are apparently at ease, and the concerned, and those for whom it has all gone beyond the reach of words.

From looking at the facts, and the firm or wavering estimates they suggest, we build, as Edwin Muir said, 'in faith and doubt our shaking house'.

Jesus did this in the way appropriate to his time and place and then turned to the world with this tremendous gift – an entirely new depth and warmth to the idea of God as Father. There are moments when it is given us to walk beside him in this, to be 'in Christ', sharing his mind, his confidence. Often, though, all we can do is take his view of things on trust.

We shall often, then, say the words 'our Father' no more than proleptically, feeling that they do not appear to be justified just now, but we have accepted Jesus as the man who knows the score and we say them now because we believe the ultimate light will show them to be the only words that meet the case.

St Luke's account of the Lord's Prayer (RSV) begins 'Father'. St Matthew's version begins 'Our Father who art in heaven'. St Luke's shorter form of the invocation, as of the whole prayer, is thought to be nearer the original that Jesus taught his friends. So Jesus may not have used the additional description 'who art in heaven', but there is no doubt at all that it is true to the mind of Jesus. He knew from the depths of himself that God is not only Father but also God.

He grew up in a tradition that naturally thought of God in human, personal terms, but at the same time was sure that God is not a man, is mysteriously much more than personal. As such he is unimaginably other than us, going about his purposes in different ways and with different thoughts from any that enter our heads.

Implicit, then, in the first words of the prayer is the thought that we must expect to be mystified by life and sometimes to be reduced to uncomprehending protest at what God does and what he allows. That protest is part of an authentic Christian spiritual life, and it ought to have its place in any worship that claims to be honest.

The rest of the Lord's Prayer, as indeed the rest of the teaching of Jesus, is a series of guidelines for people wanting to be able to see how the God who presents himself in life's disarray of encouragements and contradictions can be some kind of Father.

People who wish to arrive at that vision and are ready to follow the route suggested in this prayer are in for a struggle. They have in fact begun their own version of Jacob's wrestling with the unknown stranger in the night.

Charles Wesley's mystical poem of fourteen stanzas on that theme almost immediately struck its first readers as having an extraordinary aura of passionate and penetrating truth. The Minutes of the Methodist Conference held in London, Tuesday, 29 July 1788, recorded seven names in answer to the question as to who of 'our preachers' had died that year. Among them was, fifthly, Mr Charles Wesley, whose death, apparently so disturbing to the mind of the assembly that prose would not take the strain, was referred to with the grave quotation that for him 'the weary wheels of life stood still at last'. His poetry was then astonishingly under-acknowledged as the least praiseworthy thing about him, though this pious howler was in part redeemed by the words that follow – 'although Dr Watts did not scruple to say that "that single poem *Wrestling Jacob* was worth all the verses he himself had written" '. For equal power as a description of the essential struggle of faith there is no point in looking anywhere in English poetry except in the verse of George Herbert, Gerard Manley Hopkins, and (in our own day) R. S. Thomas.

The life of faith is a grappling with experience, my experience (not anyone else's, and certainly not that of some theoretical generality), and negotiating that nearness so that it begins to speak of God. This great poem was written by someone who knew all about that.

> Come, O thou Traveller unknown,
> Whom still I hold, but cannot see,
> My company before is gone,
> And I am left alone with thee:
> With thee all night I mean to stay,
> And wrestle till the break of day.
>
> I need not tell thee who I am,
> My misery or sin declare:
> Thyself hast called me by my name;
> Look on thy hands and read it there:
> But who, I ask thee, who art thou?
> Tell me thy name, and tell me now . . .[2]

The writer of that poem knew perfectly well that Jesus has given us a true and usable name for God. God is the Father. The special word Jesus used carried a special tenderness and affection, 'dear Father'. We are to address God in that way because our life is in fact lived within fatherly love. If you think of existence as a matter of steering your not all that seaworthy boat over the ocean of life, according to the Christian view the name of the ocean is fatherly love, and however stormy it is it is still fatherly love, and however far you drift off your course you cannot drift off the ocean. That sounds fine, but much of the time, when you are immersed in experience, it does not actually feel like that at all.

Much of the time the religious information you have been given through the pious influences of parents, teachers, the church and all the saintly examples scattered throughout its history like bright hints of God, seems to have been given you in a foreign language.

Often you are brought right to the beginning again, looking now hard at your own life almost for the first time seriously, and wondering who it is that is supposed to be hiddenly dealing with you, and how, with so little evidence in his favour, that presence can be recognized as the universal love.

That 'coming to the beginning' is important. I believe it is in part what Jesus was hinting at when he spoke about our not being able to see what he saw unless we become like children. Whatever he meant, it is certainly important to recapture some of the marvellous gravity and curiosity of youth, as it stands at the very beginning of beliefs and hopes, with everything to learn.

We can never literally begin all over again, but to be ready to learn must involve being ready to unlearn what we have wrongly learned, or at any rate to jettison what is now no longer any use.

In order to avoid the difficulty in the thought of God as the mysterious (because heavenly) Father, people tend to settle for the familiar father image and leave out the mystery.

Many English people's religious instruction virtually ended before the age of ten when they left Sunday School. Much Sunday School teaching is inevitably simplistic. It has always seemed to me to be better not to have it at all if that is all you are going to have, though I know that is not the orthodox view. Its inadequate images are a nuisance to people in later life trying to pick up where they left off in their resumed attempt to understand Christianity.

The appreciation of religion is not unlike the appreciation of music and books. Our ability to receive what they can give and to estimate their spiritual weight grows as our experience of life extends and deepens. If we are exposed to religion only in the first ten years of life it will be a thing of meagre substance and paltry meaning. On the other hand, if it becomes part of our important living, certain areas of it will grow more interesting, more needed, with the years. There then may be a similar problem at the other end. I get the impression that people in the second half of life often find it difficult to relate adequately to the local church, not because it is providing fare they cannot understand but because it is meeting needs and interests that in their case have given place to others of a different existential range.

Those who have in fact stayed with the church into adult life may find a further problem in that there is an anti-intellectual bias in much Christian preaching that ill prepares them for learning how to say 'Father' in the midst of experience that seems to mock the word.

The God the Father whom many have learned in these various ways may well have to be surrendered and replaced by a genuine faith-image of the unknown father if they are going to learn religion from Jesus.

More serious and more needing to be jettisoned is the internal image of father and authority that seems to be an important ingredient of the psychological life of many people, particularly men, whose relationship with their natural father was unsatisfactory.

A harsh father-image is often found even in men whose actual father was kindly and affectionate.

It is well known that our relationship with our father in childhood and early youth, or with father-substitutes in the formative influences of home, school or church, is important in determining whether our attitude to authority is productive or resentful, whether we are tolerant or intolerant of our own weaknesses, and whether we are going to have any confidence that we can be in some sense 'father' to the world immediately round us.

People who have negative memories of their own father are bound to have a difficult time learning to say the great prayer of Jesus.

It is not absurdly wide of the mark to see a kind of Jungian implication in the parable of the prodigal son in that there is a positive, truly creative, meaning in the son's leaving home and journeying to a far country.

The story concerns two sons who both have the mistaken idea of their father as a being who requires service and obedience. By some necessity of inner growth the younger has to leave the father he has misunderstood, and be for a time quite homeless and fatherless, in order to come, through deep experience, to being able to see his father as he really is.

The elder son never makes it. He continues to live with his mistaken view and misses everything in life that matters.

It may well be impossible to say the Lord's Prayer as though for the first time, without any preconceptions, but I am sure it is good to be wary about the spoiling deposits and misinformations of childhood and youth, and as far as possible allow God to come into one's life at first without a name of any kind.

The point of praying at all is to rid the mind of such misunderstandings and replace them with as much as truly comes home to you of the truth for which Jesus was all the time pleading.

There is a sense in which everyone has faith, and everyone behaves quite loyally and consistently with what he believes, that is to say, what he believes about himself and life. That faith, hugely important as it is, is not the sort that can be or ever is set out in a creed and spoken aloud in some ceremonial rite for all to hear. It is part of the inner life of the mind, the drift of secret thoughts whose precise character we are not sharp enough always to note but whose atmosphere we are breathing all the time.

It is the product of many ingredients – memories, wants, fears, loves both real and illusory, and also various physical satisfactions or discomforts, through all of which we interpret our life and come to some sense that things are well with us or not as well as we would like them to be.

Much of this is concealed from us, but we catch occasional glimpses of it, sometimes to our surprise or dismay. Some of it, however, is clear to our friends and people who have known us for a long time, because it has a deep and logical connection with the way we live and talk.

In our daily life we are frequently, though involuntarily and indirectly, acting out how it is with us within.

It is in that sense that our life springs from our faith and everyone is living out some kind of faith.

If we secretly believe that there is nothing much about us, that we have nothing the world particularly needs, perhaps in some dark moment that we are empty things, the odds are that we shall be driven by the need to fill our emptiness somehow. We may go through a stretch of our lives in which in one way or another we are on the make, anxiously seeking some advantage or success or recognition.

If, however, deep within where it matters, we believe that we live within the love of God, that he has created us to fulfil some part of his purpose, that he is himself within us as the ability to do or enjoy or endure what comes, we are likely to have a much more relaxed time of it. If we find life worth while we shall not need to consider the question whether we ourselves are; we shall find it rather a pointless question. As a result there will probably be enough courage in our response to life for us to be reasonably outgoing and honest.

What we really believe is the all-important matter. This is why if we want to change the way we react to events and people, it is not much use attempting to control this directly. All we shall know will be a continual running fight with the forces coming from our inner life. That fight will wear us down, no good will come of it, because we are likely to lose. The requirement for that kind of change is a change of inner faith, a new set of convictions about oneself and life, about the possibilities and the prospects.

In the Christian tradition the classical example of this process is in St Paul's journey of faith. As I understand him he seems to say that having tried hard enough to control his behaviour, only to make himself miserable with failure, he came into an entirely new range of possibility when he changed his convictions about the sort of thing God wants from us.

When he accepted Jesus' view that God wants us to embark on a relationship of trust and love with him instead of a struggle to improve ourselves, a new response to life began to form in him. It came at the deepest level, the inner world of the thoughts we most really live with, as gradually new views and expectations took root there. Eventually there are signs of this on the upper level of behaviour, though these are incidental and gracious and not the purpose of the exercise. It is just a further illustration of the principle that what is going on within gets itself acted out.

But it is always from within outward, not a set of checks and controls imposed on one's behaviour in yet one more attempt to bring it into line, but a new inner life, in his view largely the work of the divine spirit, in that region of the self where our real wants and beliefs seem to reside, and where any love, joy and peace that we are going to have will have their root.

Our part is the cultivation of the thoughts and attitudes of faith as Jesus has explained faith to us. In the life of faith people come to know God as a reality exciting them to gratitude, reverence, exasperation, love, incomprehension, joy sometimes, and much else that makes up the fullness of religious experience. It is as sure as anything in this world is sure that we shall never come to this fullness of religious experience without working for it, without deliberately cultivating the life of faith. In that work, praying has always had a prominent place.

I interpret praying fairly generously as all that you do to furnish the inner world of your secret thoughts and wants with the attitudes, trusts, likings which Jesus considered most productive of love and joy.

Praying is part of the fuller life as Jesus lived it; it serves it, extends it, and it also expresses it – sometimes more satisfactorily than any other activity can. That fuller life is mainly a matter of making progress in knowing and loving God and knowing and loving people. God and people are the most important features of reality. One wants to be in as thankful and affectionate communion with reality as possible.

As people attempt to live on the Christian assumptions, characteristic reactions to experience develop, such as pleasure, gratitude, worry, mystification, amazement, protest. These reactions need to be translated into thinkable Christian thoughts, because in this way life ceases to be a neutral affair, ceases to be an indeterminate pleasantness or frustration, and begins to radiate with Christian meaning. Prayer is one of the ways of doing that.

And all these reactions have an emotional accompaniment that needs expression and discharge. Prayer is one of the ways in which Christians and other religious people have found it good to express their feelings about life.

Praying is a very individual thing. We are most completely ourselves before God and as we try to find what life is about and what we really want from it. That means that prayer is also a journey in self-understanding. There are ways and forms of prayer hallowed by centuries of devotion that may do little for you; there are new forms that everyone is raving about that may seem to you quite ridiculous. So, one is seeking oneself as well as God when seeking God.

There is something quite unique about the Lord's Prayer. It is adequate for all occasions, however happy or terrible. For that reason it has naturally been used in private metaphor by millions crying out for this or in the face of that. Yet it carries its great load of human experience so easily it can sound utterly fresh and new in the most jaded religious or irreligious mind if its words enter there at the right moment.

It is amazing to think of the innumerable lips that have repeated it. People must revert to it so often because of its accessibility (the rest of Christianity being so remote), because it continues to clarify the shadowy longings of their hearts and turns them to what God is preparing in all the flux of experience. It is also mercifully detached from christological dogma which is such an awkward burden for the spiritual pilgrim to carry. Yet it makes clear enough Jesus' personal faith and his place in his own tradition. I do not see how it can fail to bring him into one's life.

And it is inexhaustible, deeply interesting, open to much interpretation. One way of seeing it is as a group of attitudes. If these are you, you are not likely to think that anything that matters has been left out.

Its first clause, understood with Jesus' characteristically

affectionate intonation, both excites and perturbs the mind.

The rest of the prayer can be seen as the route to that state of soul in which one can honestly call God 'Father' out of the fullness of a joyful heart.

Hallowed be thy name

THERE MUST BE very few people, if any, who find this world completely satisfying. Among various deficiencies it is unsatisfying because it does not provide the answers. Love and beauty and suffering stand in it with great dignity, but they are tantalizingly unable to explain themselves.

Jesus grew up in a tradition that made much of this common unease about the life we are given, its mixture of blessing and injury, its way of provoking and never answering the question how much any of it really matters.

From that tradition he learned to look for something better, or at any rate, something to complete it and make it at last intelligible. He seems to have been sharply conscious of the world about him and viewed it with an appreciative and discerning eye, its considerable goodness hung around as it is with so much anxiety. At the same time he continually saw another sky and another earth.

His imagination was quite possessed by the thought of the great thing he believed was soon going to happen – the coming of what he called the kingdom of God. When it arrived, it would be like a revelation; everyone would see the meaning and the glory of life, and the earth would be as full of this tremendous knowledge as the sea is full of the shift and swell of its tides.

To this is to be traced the fact that his outlook was one of peculiar gravity and joy. There is a kind of deep excitement about him (his speech loses it only rarely). It is as if, with him, anticipation has become so familiar that what he anticipates is constantly in his imagination, like footsteps heard continually coming nearer. God has actually begun to bring about this time of clearness and joy. Certainly he, Jesus himself, felt it happening in his own life.

The prayer 'hallowed be thy name' is a longing for the fullness of it, for the whole amount of that coming day when everyone will see the meaning of their lives and the world's life, and there will be gladness and reverence everywhere.

For those who pray it sincerely now, life goes on, differing of course in its pleasant and painful detail from one person to another, but the same for all in that one certainty gives it its deepest significance – that the meaning of it all, in its many shapes of good and evil, is fatherly love, and that this is going to come clear to the whole world of the living and the dead eventually.

That certainty is not vivid and powerful all the time; but to be gripped by it means to be keenly aware of the difference between life's surface and its depth. However gentle and amusing life is on the surface, in the depth of himself every honest believer knows that it is in a thousand frightful ways at present a dishonouring of much that men have come to regard as holy, and that the hope of defeating chaos continually recedes. At the same time, however horrible life may be on the surface, in the believer's prayers there is this thought of the coming joy, the great purpose completed, with humanity at last seeing God's face in gladness and needing no other light of any kind.

The prayer for the universal recognition of life's holiness

rises from this mixture of distress and hope. It is not sentimental or escapist. It is a mistake to see it as similar to the touching dream of a girl in a Tchekov play, sighing for the great compensatory rest when life will be at last tender and sweet as a caress. It is a robust state of mind, of people who see life's profanities and pains but believe them to be no more than provisional things, though calling also for our help and linked by a hidden logic to the ultimate fulfilment.

It is not, however, a mistake to see it as a prayer for the end of the world. There is a sense in which the whole of the Lord's Prayer is exactly that.

The word 'end' can mean either the last of a series or the purpose for which something exists or someone strives.

The idea of the end of time, in the sense of some last day, a final count-down to zero, is a difficult thought to put to any use, since 'last' itself implies time and seems there to suggest a contradiction. On the other hand, the thought of the end of the world as the purpose for which the world exists, as some meaning in which the earthly process comes to fulfilment, is one that many thinkers have employed. The Christian view is that the fulfilment of God's purpose as it has been explained in the teaching of Jesus is the 'end' that gives meaning to existence.

Once this thought really grips you, so that it awakens desire, and with such desire stirs memories of moments in your life whose grace you interpret as validating glimpses of its truth, you could easily imagine yourself wanting God as eagerly as some saints have wanted him.

The novelist Paul Scott describes a man so much affected by this thought that he found mere belief in it quite insufficient; he wanted in some way to press forward, to act on it, to do something about it. He not only believed in it, in a peculiar way he actually felt it. Speaking of the idea of God and heaven, he says:

> And this seemed, what? oh, such a tremendous, awful, terrible, blessed thing, such a reward, do you see, such an unfathomable state of grace that I never thought it enough to say, Yes, it is so, I believe; because if it were so then what less, yes, what less could be asked of us than to explore, to examine, to ferret it out, to spend all our short mortal time in consideration, in preparation, in pursuit of it, the idea of it, not expecting to see or actually to prove but to prepare, to establish a condition of readiness, to see all that was allowed to be seen, prove all that it was permitted to prove here on earth of what existed beyond it? I thought, how bare, how puny, how defeated to solve the equation only with faith.[1]

Some of the power of a religious idea is there. The gospels give the impression that the idea of God's kingdom produced as intense an excitement in the mind of Jesus.

'Hallowed be thy name.' To refer to God himself by the words 'thy name' has a curious indirectness, even remoteness. Actually, names and naming have a major role in the Bible.

The Genesis myth of creation describes God bringing the creatures he had made to man: 'and whatever the man called every living creature, that was its name' (Gen. 2.19).

Things are given names to establish their individuality and to distinguish them from other things. In this way experience ceases to be a random mixture. Its ingredients can be specified and organized in many complex and serviceable mental arrangements. The great naming process is language.

The Genesis story suggests that human life, the life of reasoning beings, hardly begins until man starts naming things. It begins with the word. Then almost everything else starts.

23

Poetry becomes possible, and drama, imaginative literature of all kinds, philosophy and science, conversation and humour. All that God wants man to do and enjoy implies his learning how to handle words and use them in the service of truth and love.

The importance of the word in each individual's life is unimaginably vast, if not limitless. He has to learn to name things, to identify them and bring some order into the chaos of his life, so that it begins to make some sense for him and he has some control of it.

Things have to be given their right names; and identifying means seeing clearly. In one particularly dazzling range of experience, for example, in loving, distinctions have to be made between loving and possessing, loving and dependency, loving and using, or else it all goes wrong. Indeed, love has never been easy to name correctly in the obscuring emotion that so often accompanies it. Honesty is another difficult thing to name; what looks like truthfulness is often a covert form of cruelty.

In our technological world, in which religious faith and cultural tradition no longer have significant roles, many people cannot find words for their emotional life, to clarify their experience and recognize themselves in it. They have little more than action in which to express themselves, action and things, not the feelings they generate or express. Someone has observed that if there were no cars or football many men would hardly utter a sound.

At a deeper level of our life of feeling, there are within us unidentified fears and resentments which, if only we saw them for what they are, if only we could name them, would not harrass us anywhere near as much as they do. Life is good and free, and the world is a progressive and liberated world, when whatever men and women call a thing, that is in fact its name.

Last of all in the Genesis naming story, God brings woman to man, and waits for him to name her. You become a self, Adam becomes a self, by distinguishing yourself from what is not you. To do this you have to look keenly at what is not you, register it as not you, indeed respect it as existing independently of you. Respect is a form of looking and naming, it is responsible and careful looking. When man has learned this, has named everything, learned to respect what is not him, recognize that its being is quite other than and absolutely as valid as his, he is ready for woman.

His naming of her is infinitely more complicated and protracted than his naming of things. Since what is true of him is true of her, the two halves of humanity are involved in a continual need to name to one another their characteristic wants, fears, protests, delights, so that they see each other in the heavenly light of truth. They can then in mutual understanding make all the life and love for which God created them.

This marvellously reciprocal character of love makes it the supreme means of becoming a self, and ultimately the most excellent way of knowing God.

In our century it is Martin Buber, a Jew, who has probably done most to help Christians in the West to appreciate this. He was continually saying in one way or another that it is only by saying *Thou* with the whole of one's being, without covert manipulation of others and without reservation of oneself, that one becomes an *I*.

It is part of same truth that 'not before a man can say *I* in perfect reality – that is, finding himself – can he in perfect reality say *Thou* – that is, to God'.[2]

Yet it is extraordinarily difficult to say 'Thou' to another human being, to let him be freely himself, in his current need or enthusiasm. We have designs on him, even before we meet him. When he comes into our presence he comes into no open, free space but into a constricted area of demand.

We treat time in the same way. Each day most of us do not waken to a new day, to a fresh thing that at once excites our interest and trust. We had something of a struggle with bits of yesterday, and of the day before, and its predecessor. A kind of being on guard has become habitual with us. We do not notice that when we wake we sense difficulty in the air, and before we put on our clothes we assume such protection for our hearts as we have acquired over the years. The first person who comes into our presence comes, not as himself simply, but as one whom we need in some way or even vaguely fear. We have difficulty in letting him be himself.

Yet he may be in deepest need. Everyone knows that the ability to realize what another person is actually *feeling* in a given situation is at the heart of true understanding. That is difficult to achieve if our own feelings are in the way.

Even in deepest love two people still look at each other through the misty glass of their own feelings. When two people marry, their past is alive and well and living at their new address. In one it may take the form of the remembered beauty of some part of his childhood which he hopes to recover, in the other it may be some deprivation in the past which pleads for compensation. All of us are to some extent living with ghosts of ourselves, real enough to influence the expectations we have of other people and prevent us seeing the truth about how things are with them.

Appreciating this tendency in us all to project our own needs on to others is a strenuous part of learning how to love another human being, how to let his or her 'name', that is to say, his or her self as it is just now, *be*, in its sacred legitimacy and freedom.

It is even more important in learning how to love God. 'Hallowed by thy name' means not only that we want the world's recognition and acknowledgment of him, it means letting God be what he chooses to be.

From childhood Jesus drew a deep sense of this from his spiritual tradition. His people seem to have wanted to keep their imaginations alert to the mystery and otherness of God, and for this reason they did not allow any material representations of God in religion or art, forbade even the pronouncing of God's name. It was a curious name. Its discernment was one of the most crucial moments in their journey of faith.

> Then Moses said to God, 'If I come to the people of Israel and say to them, "The God of your fathers has sent me to you", and they ask me, "What is his name?", what shall I say to them?' God said to Moses, 'I am who I am.' And he said, 'Say this to the people of Israel, "I am has sent me to you" (Ex. 3.13f.).

This famous passage has a footnote in the Revised Standard Version which explains that the name can be just as satisfactorily translated 'I am what I am', or, 'I will be what I will be'. So that the name amounted almost to a namelessness, as though there is the realization that whatever we may learn about God we must never limit God by descriptions and predictions.

Martin Buber interprets the name in this way:

> 'I shall be there as he who I there shall be.' He is ever there, ever present to his creature, but always as he who is just here and now; the spirit of man cannot foretell in what garment of what being and what situation God will be manifested. It is for man to recognise him in each of his garments.[3]

27

We can come to think we know a little of what God is, and that what we are currently enjoying or enduring has a place in life's meaning, but we can never know who or what God is in himself. We believe he speaks and gives himself in some way in everything that happens. We are always in his presence. Religion is for many of us, though not for all, our principal means of deepening our awareness of that and learning how to live with it, not afraid of it or oppressed by it, but free to lament and love in faith. We may have to say, with St Augustine and many others, that we know what God is not but unfortunately cannot yet say what he is.

It has been said that religion is Isaiah, Jesus, Paul, Augustine, Francis, Luther, and all that sort of thing, with more that each of us finds for himself. That is a ridiculously narrow Christian list, though what it means to convey is fine – that all those, and countless others the world over, and we ourselves, have in one way and another found the goodness and glory of life, its unexpected opportunities, its undeserved rescues and forgivenesses, and given it the kind of gratitude and praise one does not give to the merely human.

In various ways most people are struggling with the presence. We wonder how much of life is our own responsibility, how much simply the play of circumstance, whether in it something important is being done or prepared or perhaps paid for. Such words stand up for a while but soon collapse on the floor of the mind. Still, people brooding over such matters are functioning religiously, even if just now they resent such an honorific view of the mess in their minds.

We live in a time when it is conventional to be hugely sensitive about using the word 'God' at all. I suppose that behind that sensitiveness is the fear of being regarded as accepting that notable word's unpleasant accretions, since much that is ridiculous, much that is terrible, has been done in the name of God. There may also be the admirably sharp recognition that it is so easy to make the word a substitute for, or an evasion of, the presence it names. But there is no other word.

Martin Buber has told how he once tried to reply to someone with this deep reluctance about using the word 'God'. He admitted that the word has been soiled and mutilated more than any other word, but he argued:

> . . . just for this reason I may not abandon it. Generations of men have laid the burden of their anxious lives upon this word and weighed it to the ground . . . The races of man with their religious factions have torn the word to pieces; they have killed for it and died for it, and it bears their finger-marks and their blood.

But, he maintained, no other word will do. When anyone uses it he does in fact mean by it that reality that generations of men have both honoured and degraded. And when in their loneliest darkness of genuine need they sigh or cry the word 'God', it is in fact the living God whom they implore.

> And just for this reason is not the word 'God', the word of appeal, the word which has become a *name*, consecrated in all human tongues for all times?[4]

In Jesus' use of this name, he who is, who will be what he will be, is for ever 'our Father'. So, to pray 'hallowed be thy name' is now to want that fatherhood recognized and acknowledged, both by vindicating itself and by being loved freely in an honest world.

There are many who still hesitate over this use of the personal.

Yet what in human experience is at one and the same time

mysterious, vital, unplayable with, and yet beautiful, responsive, lovable? Nothing so much as persons, or perhaps one person, or even one imagined and never to be attained person. The goodness and depth of life seem to affect us in similar fashion, while in no sense being actually a person. It seems natural that Jesus should pick his name for God from that realm.

People who still have trouble with it can at any rate reflect that there is time. A faith takes time to gather and grow. If one cannot yet use this word 'Father', one can at least say a simple, unqualified 'Thou' to the goodness and glory of life, and let the other side of what goes on in prayer fill that vacant 'Thou' with many meanings, slowly, through all the time it takes, as one goes on longing for the world to be a whole, where no one is ever deluded by happiness, and pain is never allowed to run to waste, and he who is even now in every situation has at last erased from our hearts all principles that are not the motions of love.

Thy kingdom come, thy will be done, on earth as it is in heaven

SOME PEOPLE MAKE sense of life by thinking about all the courage and achievement of the generations. Endless waves of injustice have swept over them, yet human tenderness is never entirely washed away. Between recurring periods of violence, sometimes during their fury, civilizing effort goes forward, creates beautiful things, improves conditions, renews hope in the inexhaustible human spirit. Under the influence of these cheering facts there are still a few people outside the USSR (where it is political orthodoxy) who think that humanity is slowly, admittedly painfully, but surely, moving towards some kind of ideal society. This prospect is thought to give our lives the meaning that justifies the effort we put into them.

Jesus did not think that way at all. It is not possible to find in his words any hint that he looked forward to the gradual elimination of evil in a universal peace and order that some future generation would enjoy. No kind of this-worldy futurism would have made any sense to him. His mind was occupied with the ultimate and with now, with heaven and earth.

The contrast between them shakes the mind. Heaven is the

realm of God's being, and the holiness, truth, life that are forms of his glory. Earth is what we know, the scene of our conflicts and perplexities, of satisfactions of our wants and assaults on our weakness, though, we think, with signals and signs from heaven continually lighting things up.

These signs and signals, coming most obviously in the experiences we most deeply value but by no means confined to them, are sometimes clear and sometimes so ambiguous that decoding them is a very uncertain exercise; but they are all, when interpreted by the faith of Jesus, indications of the coming of the kingdom of God, as the monitory flashes of light on a sultry evening anticipate the downpour of life-giving rain on the way.

This coming kingdom of God is no future harmony that we are slowly building. It is the complete victory over evil and the revelation of what joy really is that amounts to the supreme hallowing of God's name, everyone at last, with relief and delight, seeing that he is God. It is part of the realism of Jesus that that is obviously not something that human beings are ever going to achieve. It is his huge faith that God will do it. What is given to us is to believe with Jesus that God will indeed do it, and to immerse ourselves in all that follows from that belief.

It follows from believing in the coming new world that we shall naturally and happily hope for it. If we hope for it, we shall pray for it; indeed hopes are in fact prayers, because where your hope is there will your heart be also, whatever your superficial self is saying with its lips.

If we hope for it, something is bound to happen in our disorganized and inconsistent selves. There is a kind of life that must necessarily grow from this hope (however long it takes) as naturally as a plant owes its particular grace to its constituting seed. There will be the gradual emergence of actions and reactions that are the expression of this continual looking to the Father and longing for the fulfilment he is preparing.

It will be part of the same process that our failures will become more painful. They will not be just failures, they will be experiences of being torn in two.

Also, attached to believing in the coming kingdom, though it is a very tricky business setting this down in words that do not at some point, some depth, irritate one's religious mind, there is the possibility that we shall be among those who by God's grace actually enter the kingdom. There are people for whom it has been prepared, as a piece of music is made for the people who will play it.

To the question who they are there can be only a partial, open-ended answer. If there was a clear answer we should all divide immediately into the confident and the despairing. All that can be said is that Jesus spoke at length about this and left us a group of mental pictures that have haunted the Christian world's spiritual life like presences.

It appears that the people for whom the great fulfilment is prepared are merciful in their moral assessments, forgiving in their injuries, able to make some positive use of suffering.

He hinted also that the kingdom's presence is proclaimed by humility, openness, affection, trust, and the sudden generosity of a thankful heart.

He was certainly drawn to the weak and sensual and broken who know it and long to see life changed into something that will make up for the wasted years, and to those who wait for someone in whose presence they can put down a tremendous burden they have been carrying all their lives.

The list is never exhausted. There is never unanimous agreement about who are in it. One thing is clear. If you put together all his images of what is ultimately acceptable, in no sense is it a

33

list of qualifying achievement, making a set of 'shoulds' to which we have to measure up; it is simply a series of pointers to the meaning for him of this term 'the kingdom of God'. It is always God's gift to a certain kind of receptiveness. It is often surprising and unexpected, and inevitably it is occasionally thought to be quite outrageous.

So, again and again, in the gospels Jesus is seen confronting the despairing, to tell them they need not think that they are finished, and the confident, to persuade them to think again. And those who receive Jesus' commendation do not impress us as winners or earners – that could make us envious or hopeless – but simply people who make clear the meaning of the kingdom, giving us anticipations of its style, confirmations of its desirability, and make us ask for more of it.

Jesus' thoughts about what is ultimately acceptable, what will ultimately prevail, have not had any serious challenge from any other ideas about how best to fill the time between the cradle and the grave. The ambitious idea of the gradual improvement of the human condition that is the inspiration of the various forms of humanism, while agreeable to most of us in our extroverted moods, does not meet our deeper questions. There is little in the contemporary scene to encourage us to think that our generation represents the highest point of progress so far and that the light is brightening all round us. Nor is there any scientific basis for the assumption that the earth is immortal and destined to carry its freight of human life for ever.

What is more, any point of view which puts the meaning of the human journey at the journey's end inevitably depreciates the journey, is unforgiveably heartless to those who fall *en route*, and endows an imaginary last generation with an irrational prestige.

Raymond Chandler wrote excellent detective stories and also

had interesting ideas on the form. He points out[1] that the standard detective story is unsatisfactory because it is based on the assumption that murder will out and justice will be done. Technically it takes for granted the relative insignificance of everything except the final *dénouement*. What leads up to that is what he calls 'more or less passage-work'. The *dénouement* justifies everything. He learned from an intelligent film producer that it is impossible to make a successful film from that kind of story because then 'the whole point is a disclosure that takes a few seconds of screen time while the audience is reaching for its hat'. He came to see that the true mystery is one in which the individual scene carries almost as much weight as the plot, in the sense that a good plot makes good scenes. The ideal mystery is 'one you would read if the end was missing'.

Like Chandler's ideal mystery, human life, as Jesus understood it, is not that brand of story whose meaning is entirely concentrated in some eschatological disclosure and explanation. All our moments, all life's scenes, are packed with importance, but they are also in meaning and purpose related to an end. They are encounters with God, who is always present grace for the doing of his will and is he who will ultimately be glorified in the reconciliation of heaven and earth. And when we pray 'thy kingdom come, thy will be done, on earth as it is in heaven' we are asking for the knowledge of his will for us in the present situation and for help to do it, and we are also praying that he will admit us into the final reconciliation of things, not assessing our merits, which are decidedly thin, but amply pardoning us.

This view of things is not for everyone. There are people who are not continually nudged by the need to refer all that they experience to some rational meaning, comprehensive in its scope. They manage to find life on the whole one reasonably interesting scene after another, not needing to be translated into some memorable insight, and they are not disturbed by the fact that for them the end of the mystery is missing. Growing older, they find religious argument tedious and their intellectual curiosity fading, as they realize (with Graham Greene) that now 'one hasn't long to wait for revelation or darkness'.[2]

Others think that there is something astonishing about our admittedly limited presence in this world, and sense this with increasing conviction, if not precision, as they grow older. I do not believe that these are in any way better than the others. Lives can have meaning and worth without a formulated religious faith. It is one of the facts of life that there are different ways of being in the world, each with its special intensity and value.

In the great religious tradition whose textbook is the Bible, ideas play an enormous part – descriptions of God, estimates of Jesus, explanations of human failure and divine dilatoriness, forecastings of some sort of conclusion. But meaning is not necessarily associated with ideas. People can participate fully in life's richness without any conscious faith, finding stimulation and self-expression in many important purposes and interests, and accumulating sufficient tolerance and imagination to cope with the normal misfortunes.

The mental world that Jesus inhabited was of the other kind. It was a world of certain tremendous presences and ideas.

Those who look in gratitude to him have always tried to live with a comprehensive view of the human condition in which each scene of the mystery is intriguing, but not self-sufficient, since it is related to a *dénouement* to come.

That fulfilment is beyond time, and so by definition ineffable, but in certain attitudes and acts we believe its attraction can be felt. There are happinesses, endurances, deliverances that are understood as bearing its grace; and what happened in and around Jesus of Nazareth is so ablaze with its light that in him the kingdom is virtually here. 'If I by the finger of God cast out devils, then the kingdom of God has come upon you' (Luke 11.20). Every Christian has his own list of experiences in which he believes he sees the dawn light of the coming day, but all of them, and everyone's put together, 'hints and guesses, hints followed by guesses', add up to no more than faith.

If we pray for the coming of God's kingdom and live in anticipation of its coming, we find ourselves wanting to live lives that correspond. Our 'thy will be done' carries not only the desire that God will do the great final thing he intends but also our wish to do his will here and now as long as there is a here and now.

The doing of God's will is always some form of the hallowing of his name. It is an acknowledgment of his goodness, and so an earnest of that acknowledgment of his goodness that ultimately will flood the whole universe. As Jesus unpacked this great idea it turned out to be a matter of loving God and one's neighbour.

He summarized the moral tradition in which he grew up in two commandments that join these two forms of love insepar- ably together. He believed that life is for loving God with every capacity and energy of our being, and loving our neighbour as a person in every desire, fear, regret, impatience just like ourselves.

It has frequently been asked whether these two loves are in fact two or one and the same thing.

So, it has sometimes been pleaded that there is only one love. It stirs everyone, so that no one should be written off as hope- less. It is the love of God. All other loves are forms of the love of God in some way failing to be its true self, or settling (usually unconsciously) for less than it really wants and is meant to have.

The peculiar incompleteness in most loves, and their exquisite pain, which is ironically part of their seduction, is to be traced to the fact that in the love of material things what is loved may well seem perfect but is incapable of answering, of saying Yes to us, while in the love of persons what is loved can respond but is always imperfect.

All human loving, from the highest down to the most disordered or depraved, is really the human heart shaken with longing for that ultimate perfection which is also the perfect lover.

I have always thought that this is a way of understanding love and life that is very appealing, though I can see that it involves the risk that earthly loves may be rated less than their true worth. If there is something mistaken and extreme about it, I am sure that even so the world can do with plenty of that exaggeration, because most people find that life suffers more from mediocrity and cynicism than from the longing for perfection.

Today it is more fashionable to say that there is only one love, and it is the love of neighbour. God is spirit. He cannot be seen, heard, touched. We can love him only in a mediated fashion, by loving that which we can in fact see, hear and touch, and particularly the hungry and imprisoned characters who walk this maladjusted world in such tragic numbers.

I have never been satisfied with either idea. No one is going to disagree that the important thing in life is how much loving gets done, and particularly how much loving people gets done. But I am sure that the religion of Jesus is a religion and not just a morality, not just a plea for a certain kind of behaviour, even loving behaviour. When it is reduced to a plea for love, it is astonishing how reduced it is, how it just takes its place, not outstandingly, along with several other great statements of humanity's vision of love as the great rescuer of all that has fallen.

By a religion I mean all that follows from seeing one's life, all life, all that is known about anything and everything, in terms of the thought of God. I think, too, of religion's gift of both magnifying your awareness of the world, of what is happening round you, and also encouraging you to begin the inner journey of an interested mind, the journey to self-understanding and the release of one's pent-up love.

On this view it is a misunderstanding of these sensitive matters to say that to love God is the same thing as loving one's neighbour. To love God is primarily to feed and develop this characteristically religious view of life, by reflection and sacramental celebration, by allowing the thought of God to go where it wants to go until you realize its range is infinite, by being willing that it should not remain a thought but become truly a presence, a presence that has power which you may resist but cannot deny.

T. S. Eliot said of certain poets that they were not just thinkers but really felt their thought 'as immediately as the odour of a rose'. Their thought was much more than a rational affair, it was an experience that modified their sensibility. That unmistakable feeling of reality, the note of truth and vitality, comes and goes in human experience very variously. There is no better dimension of life in which to observe this than the world of religion. In those moments or experiences in which God is a real presence you are quite certain that the worship of God is infinitely more than the service of mankind.

It is certainly part of the Christian experience that as the sense of God grows, it will reduce self-preoccupation and release compassion in the most injured or exhausted heart. When that happens, however, it is secondary, it is a result of the deeper

39

thing, not part of its definition. Indeed, it is possible to be intensely religious and have a comparatively weak feeling for goodness, just as there are profoundly humble and merciful people who cannot make any use at all of the word 'God'.

When Christian religious experience produces loving, it seems generally to be a kind of offshoot of joy.

This suggests that loving one's neighbour is not just a matter of loving one's neighbour. It is being able to love many things other than one's neighbour; it is the result of a grateful deepening of one's love of life itself. If you only love your neighbour, you will not love your neighbour for long. Your dissatisfaction with the rest of life will erode the goodwill that carries you to your neighbour; or else it will put a strain of anxiety into your loving, as though you are trying to justify something, or are making up in the outer world for being in some way undernourished within.

It does seem that it is loving, rather than specifically loving one's neighbour, that is the issue, being able to love and enjoy generously, and to look back thankfully to past joy and forward expectantly to more. Though there are some people who have a marvellous gift of loving, with most of us our loving requires a certain atmosphere in which to breathe with any freedom, a view of life and its meaning and prospects that encourages us to take experience in an interested and affectionate way and helps us to regain this orientation when we lose it through one pressure or another.

Loving God, in the Christian view, is that kind of thing. It is to be concerned with the meaning of life and its possibilities as these have been explained to us by Jesus, to increase our hold on that meaning, to be glad about the confirming clues we come across, so that our secret fight with life comes to a truce and we find that increasingly we approve of the way things go. When that happens, our loving tends to be released too.

Two incidents in the New Testament can be taken as particularly encouraging these ideas. Both concern women. There are so many signs that God has given women a special insight into the place of worship in life that one is inclined to assume unconscious anxiety behind the persistent tendency of men, and particularly churchmen, to see them as coming into their own primarily in various forms of service, of love of neighbour.

In one, a meal is in progress and Jesus is one of the guests (Mark 14.3–9). A woman comes in carrying some perfume which, apparently in floods of tears, she pours over him, to the general surprise and embarrassment. The result is rather odd. There are high-minded mutterings, not about the impropriety of it but the waste. There is the mean and dingy argument that it would have been far better if the perfume had been sold and the money given to the poor.

Jesus will not have the woman attacked, and he defends her handsomely:

Let her alone . . . she has done a beautiful thing to me. For you always have the poor with you, and whenever you will you can do good to them; but you will not always have me.

Jesus was certainly not unsympathetic to the poor. He is, in fact, the principle image in the Western mind for that kind of compassion. What concerns him here seems to be that certain actions are appropriate to certain situations.

The world being what it is, there will always be poor to be relieved. Not that that kind of talk is any help to the poor, but that that is our kind of world.

This particular situation, however, had a special significance for this woman. It appears from the other accounts of the

41

incident (it comes in all four gospels) that she wanted to say her thanks for some sort of release that he had apparently brought her.

She can be imagined as a woman who for quite a long time had not expected much from people. Their nearness was worth no more than their remoteness. She was not able to rid herself of her sense of life's disgrace.

Then she met Jesus, and found that he had felt the disgrace of things too. (Someone said that he had been 'made sin' on our behalf.) With that kind of understanding, he helped her to emerge from her mental gloom into the light he saw poured over everything. Part of herself that she had devalued or lost entirely was restored to her, and with immense relief she began to see that all her depression amounted to a ridiculous under-estimation of life and its prospects.

And she could not find words or tone of voice for the gratitude she felt. So one day she went looking for Jesus, found him in a rather respectable house, and did what she did. Perhaps she also wanted to express her feelings about Jesus himself, loving him and mysteriously sensing that he was a doomed figure, the centre of some obscure tragedy.

Anyway, it was for her a loaded situation, compelling her to pour all her feeling about him into this one act of grateful love as the only chance she might ever have of doing any such thing.

Such acts are often extremely beautiful. They have in them the essence of love, of art, of any religion capable of inspiring anyone. And they are quite useless, or at any rate seem so, in the sense that they cannot be made use of, they do not appear to contribute to life. Practical voices will always be raised questioning what good has been done.

There are people who see religion as justified only as a tool for some other purpose, as a means of keeping young people good or preserving marriage and the family or shoring up some other side of the shaky structure of morality. They stand among the murmurers at this never-to-be-forgotten meal.

In Canterbury there was recently an appeal for three million pounds for the preservation of the Cathedral. It is muddled thinking to set such an appeal against the need of the poor of the world, or even the considerable need for housing in Canterbury. Religion and the good of man cannot be opposed in some scale of values, because religion *is* man.

It is certainly the case that without religion, as a source of meaning and compassion, the poor of the world, and the needy generally, will have the less going for them; but it is not the justification of religion or anything in it that it is the source of moral inspiration. Human beings have never weighed up the advantages and disadvantages of religion on the basis of some cost-benefit assessment and decided that it will be worth it to go in for God. Mankind cannot help wanting God. That is the sort of being man is.

Human beings cannot live by the immediately useful alone; they need the sacramental, they need life's depth and the depth in themselves signified and addressed. Indeed it is only if they are willing to explore the depth and mystery of experience that people's lives remain interesting as the years pass and make what is left in the cup begin to look meagre.

The other New Testament incident also concerns unacceptable behaviour at a meal (Luke 10.38–42). Jesus was invited to a meal by two sisters. One of them apparently saw in him not just a friend but a mysterious man of God, someone in touch with the truth about life, who knew how to give all life's interests and anxieties their due rating.

Again it is a question of what is appropriate to the situation. The chance might never come again of hearing and questioning this charismatic figure. He himself knew that there was not much time, but there was always time on his hands apparently for talk about what matters, such as why so much is wrong and why what is right is so beautiful. She sits at his feet.

Her sister gets the meal ready. She may well have been the more devout of the two, and naturally resentful, and envious of her sister. She simply lacked spiritual imagination, and on this occasion failed to see the relative importance of things like food and drink, and even the needs of the man of Nazareth, when the Presence, the holy, the one really interesting thing in religion, has come into your house.

The argument is not that this is particularly admirable, or that people who do not register this dimension of life are inferior. It is beyond goodness and badness. It is, however, what religion is centrally about. It is not the only thing that religion is 'about'; it is, nevertheless, that good part of religion that will never be taken from it, never become obsolete.

The prayer 'thy kingdom come, thy will be done' is the same kind of thing. It is a longing for the ultimate satisfaction when heaven and earth will be reconciled and we ourselves shall no longer be the perplexed and ambivalent creatures that we are, pulled in two different ways, but there will be one universe of joy and God will be all in all.

We have anticipations of it in various kinds of deliverance, rightness, loving, that are the intermittent light of our lives. It is in this sense that Jesus spoke of the kingdom as not only to come but coming here and now, being within us, or on the point of coming, or waiting outside every situation for its chance to come. Consequently, it is also, as he explained, something you can miss, something you can fail to notice, something for which you can be for some reason just too late.

It is not less real for being only a partial affair, nor less to be welcomed because we believe that ultimately we shall fully know, as completely as God knows us now. The briefest experience of it is of the light of the kingdom.

It is in this way that the prayer 'thy will be done' is properly used in the present situation, whatever it is, even if – indeed especially if – it is one of disaster or injustice or terrible waste.

It has sometimes been used in a backward-looking sense. 'Your will has been done; we accept what has happened as coming from you; we cannot really do otherwise; rebellion and resentment are not going to help us; we accept.'

Jesus did not mean the words in that sense. For him the meaning was forward-looking and active – may God's will be done, throughout the whole scheme of things, and particularly here and now, in this that is happening now.

They were never a pious or resigned comment on what has already happened.

The Lord's Prayer, said in a time of disappointment or grief, does not carry any statement about where the pain has come from or why it has come. We are saying: now that this has come, we want to know, as much as we can know, what you wish us to do in it and with it. There is bound to be something productive to be done in it and with it, and we hope thet we shall not be so resentful or fearful that we cannot see it and do it, even if it is little more than the acquisition of experience and the extension of our acquaintance with grief.

Since it is part of a full life to know sorrow at first hand, the receiving of the abundant life of Jesus will include that. It will also include the associated experience of making fears and frustrations points of growth, because most people find that they seem to grow more, receive more, in negotiating life's ill than in enjoying its good. It is very much to be doubted whether unalloyed pleasure, pleasure that is not associated with some kind of effort and patience, contributes anything to life except as a form of relaxation and play. It is certain that pleasures, in whatever quantity, can never produce joy. In great quantity they always produce boredom.

The doing of God's will is usually a matter of fulfilling already accepted responsibilities in our daily work and personal relationships, of tolerating what in one's life cannot at present be altered, and of appreciating the enjoyable and enjoying it to the full.

In the more complex problems of life, doing God's will will be whatever loving, trusting, hoping we are capable of, having begun to 'learn Christ' and also of course having so much more to learn. Jesus gives little specific guidance for us in particular situations. He seems to have been concerned with the inwardness rather than the outwardness of behaviour. He wanted people to appreciate the subtleties and obscurities of motive, to be clear about what a ridiculous thing pride is, and for the rest to be open and imaginatively sympathetic.

There are definite points in his teaching, but on the whole it does not strike one as remarkably clear. Perhaps this was deliberate. Sets of rules easily become defences against loving imaginatively; they tend to foreclose moral discussion that ought to continue.

If we are willing to learn what is involved in loving, what God can do and cannot do, how to reduce the fear and complaint and increase the trust in our life, we do make progress. But it is progress in religious joy rather than in awareness of skilful or right performance.

The word 'love' is, of course, used extensively in Christian comment, as indeed it is in other traditions of religious and non-religious idealism. It is a word that remains an empty shell until it is given meaning and form. When it is given meaning and form in particular instances it is often the subject of disagreement and debate.

St Paul told his friends how keenly he wished that their loving might grow in factual knowledge and imaginative insight and so acquire discernment (Phil. 1.9). It looks as if right from the start it was realized that considerable work is involved in learning what shape Christian love should take in this or that situation.

There may then be characteristically Christian forms of loving, different from others, though no more admirable. Similarly, there will be characteristic failures into which Christians will fall, and harm they will do, as the difficulty of the task proves too much for them at times.

It is good to acknowledge that we are simply trying to discern God's will and do it, that we see this in terms of the love and religious vision that we observe in Jesus, and that this is an exercise both fascinating and risky.

Nowadays there is no longer any accepted pattern of good which all people of goodwill are trying to achieve. Because of that it is much to be desired that all of us, Christians and non-Christians, both separately and in sympathetic discussion, should think out a set of ideals and proprieties that will keep the community in working order while allowing as much freedom as possible. There is no resting-point in banalities like 'all you need is love', though it might be said that the work could begin there.

Some areas of life are in a particularly uncertain and disturbed condition just now, as though subterranean forces are stirring in our common life and a kind of volcanic change is in process. How relations between the government and the trade unions can be ordered to provide the most productive mutual stimulation, what is good and what is dangerous in the split between the generations and how best they can enrich one another's

47

emotional life, what conditions and behaviour are most likely to give sexual love new freshness and fulfilment as well as stability – these are just examples of several questions that make life particularly interesting at present.

I do not believe that, as compared with other thinkers, Christians have anything specially authoritative to say about God's will in these sensitive matters. They share the excitement and the perplexity of the times. They stand in unprivileged co-operation with those of other faiths and none as far as technical knowledge of any problem is concerned. What distinguishes them is the enthusiasm and hope that come from faith, from their obsession with a 'kingdom' that is, and is to come, and is at hand whenever images of birth and love and death stir the mind.

Give us this day our daily bread

THERE COULD NOT BE a simpler and more straightforward request than 'give us today our daily bread'. That must be the popular view of this part of the prayer. Actually, on the lips of Jesus, the request is not simple at all. It is not what it seems.

He cannot have meant ordinary bread, or bread as a comprehensive image for food in general. It was an important part of his teaching that one should not be anxious about food. He taught his friends to regard as the staff of life not bread, but what God says, in all life's magnificence and perplexing detail.

As for the view that the idea of bread is meant to suggest the world of work and its due reward, that simply does not sound like Jesus. He recommended that people see the point of their work not as procuring daily bread, the bread that can go stale, but some, obviously spiritual, thing that he called the bread of life (Matt. 4.4; 6.31; John 5.27).

There are important matters that we want to pray about, that surely need to be held regularly in the mind as it tries to maintain its spiritual bearings, but daily bread is not one of them, though it is part of life's goodness and need. It is like money, not an obvious subject for prayer. God has none of either to give us.

What about the people who have no bread, the world's poor

and oppressed and underprivileged, on whom has been laid the iniquity of us all? There would be far more sense in their asking God for help in planning a revolution than in praying for bread, ordinary bread.

In the Greek Testament, the word translated 'daily' means literally 'of the coming day', 'of tomorrow'. The word translated 'this day' comes at the end of the sentence, deliberately, for emphasis. So it is a mysterious request. 'Our bread of tomorrow give us – today.'

For Jesus, 'tomorrow' meant normally, of course, the day that follows this day; but there was another tomorrow that excited his imagination with far more urgency. It was the day when God will complete his purpose and be understood and acknowledged as who he tremendously is, to the endless joy of the whole creation.[1]

That tomorrow represented so much of his faith and longing that it virtually monopolized the meaning of the word 'tomorrow'. Even the word 'today' had something of the light of The Day on it, so that sometimes today would have seemed comparatively unimportant, a shadow hiding the one that really matters.

He had learned through his religious tradition to think of the great fulfilment under the image of a happy feast to which they would come from all the four corners of the earth to sit down together at God's table, all questions and resentments vanished. Naturally, then, the regular, ordinary eating and drinking of daily life began to be graced with a feeling of anticipation. For Jesus, an ordinary meal was a congenial sign of the coming kingdom, when the 'living bread', the presence of God, will satisfy everyone and bind divided humanity together in a love this world has never seen.

It is the living bread that is being asked for in this prayer.

That is why the emphatic, terminal 'today' balances the mysterious 'of tomorrow'. Grant us now, this very day, the sense of that holy day when all will be satisfied with that which alone truly meets human desire and need. Grant us here and now the joy and affection of that time, and its sense of God, as much as it is possible for them to be enjoyed here and now and by people like us.

Obviously we cannot have the whole amount of it now. We are creatures of time as well as eternity. We stand near enough to be touched by the ultimate kingdom, but are not yet quite within it. We ask for the feel of its glory, the taste of it.

So, we are not asking that the material needs of our bodies shall be met, though that is a natural thing to ask of life. It is in fact such a natural request that Jesus more or less dismissed it – not in the sense that it is unimportant or that spiritually minded people should somehow strive to be above it, but because it is so important that we take it as read ('your heavenly Father knows that you have need of all these things', Matt. 6.32). The point is that we do not consider it a major concern of spoken prayer.

Nor are we asking that the needs of the poor of the world shall be met. Christian love knows that the meeting of those needs is not something we ask God for, but something he asks us for.

We are asking essentially for that which is the point and object of religion, for God himself now and hereafter, for what Jesus called the bread of life.

All of which, so uncompromisingly stated, raises the question of its truth for us, whether we do in fact want God as much as that. Much of the time I would have to say No; because much of the time I am not *dans le vrai*, not in the truth about life and about myself.

Consequently, I would never dream of investing all moments with the same authority.

Occasionally, however, there are moments of quite exceptional radiance that seem to carry extraordinary power and meaning. Their importance is out of all proportion to their infrequency, and their influence extends far beyond their duration. They excite the desire for God; and this desire persists, and I am glad it does, and I encourage it with bits of discipline. As a result, life goes much better, I am conscious of it going less agitatedly, with greater interest and to more satisfactory purpose, and I want him the more. He is not an aid, to be dispensed with when conditions improve. 'The devil was ill, the devil a monk would be' is a bit of ancient wisdom that has always seemed nonsense to me. One never wants God in misery. As this world's light increases, his flame burns brighter.

I believe, too, something that all priests and ministers will find familiar, because my work has opened up to me the sight of so much human unhappiness and defeat, that such things are not going to have the last word in any life. I believe in the destruction of hell. And once you get into this range of conviction you find the language of religion the language you want to speak. I am far too sceptical to believe that the long process of history and the pathos of each individual's fragment of it have no more purpose than the random bursting of bubbles in a glass. Anyone playing about with that idea will soon be restless with any interpretation of life other than a religious one. Of the religious ones I have never wanted any other image than the sacrifice of Christ, as that stupendous thing is unfolded in the belief, ceremonial, prayer, ill-success of the Christian church.

To return to special moments of insight or illumination; sometimes there is an absolute quality in them that makes whatever you are doing, and indeed life itself, seem quite secondary.

Something occurs that robs the whole bag of tricks of every vestige of importance, and you want this reality to which your faith gropes and your prayers ascend – just for itself; not for pragmatic reasons or because it satisfies 'the blessed rage for order' but just for itself. I regard these rare moments of simply wanting God as infinitely precious. I have no evidence at all that they have ever done me the slightest bit of good; but they always end with an extraordinary sense that it is not wrong to want in that way, that as such one is 'in the truth'.

The only other times when I approach this peculiar state of wanting God are when listening to certain music or looking at certain paintings that have moved me so often that they now carry not only their own meaning as far as I can grasp it but also a considerable part of my own life, so that my appreciation of them is like plunging into a very deep sea indeed.

Most people have glimpses of perfection like these, when the picture or the music or whatever it is seems to become transparent and for a brief time they know an amazing widening of consciousness that makes them hungry for more of this life. Generally, however, as soon as you have registered this 'beyond' and registered it as infinitely desirable, it is as though (as Keats described it) a bell sounds to toll you back to your sole self. Our faith is that one of the meanings of the kingdom of God is that we shall not always have to put up with that inevitable return. There is to be not only the grasping of what we have loved with the best part of ourselves, but the holding of it for ever.

Meanwhile, Christians live in the world of today, though with a strong sense of this astonishing tomorrow. That is what is meant by the hallowing of life. It is not, of course, necessary that life should be hallowed in this way. It can be lived intelligently, with unselfishness and admirable purpose, without being referred, in prayer or belief, to the thought of God or of any other world than this. Such a life is not less wise or noble for being 'secular' like that.

The difference between a holy and a secular life is certainly not one of superior ethical standards. The word 'holy' is used of things, places, persons, experiences, that are thought to have a special meaning derived from the presence of God. Life itself is hallowed as the 'secular' world is brightened, disturbed, enlarged by the holy, by hints and signs of the presence of God.

The prayer for bread is a request that the meaning and affection of the coming great day of God, all its happiness and delight in each other, may be present and active in some, necessarily partial, form today.

'Today' is life in the broken kingdoms of this world, where the whole truth is rarely spoken, both sacred and profane love fall into patterns of dullness, and there is no evidence that human pain is one suffering less than it was two thousand years ago. All this, Jesus said, can nevertheless be lit with the radiance of God.

The Christian church has been working out ever since what he could mean, what sort of a life would actually be lived by someone nourished on the bread of heaven, living in the light of the coming Day. Christian holiness is the story of that, of incessant interpretations and re-interpretations, in word and life, of what it means to love God and man.

One of the most interesting of these interpretations is that which has taken the form of the monastic vows of poverty, chastity and obedience. It has certainly had a dramatic role in Christian spirituality.

These vows bear endless examination, simply because they represent a brave and persistent attempt to show what love must essentially be, and so they are guidelines (if not the only ones) for all Christians, whatever their vocation. The training and ordering of the mind to make it an instrument of loving will always involve dispositions clearly related to this classical model of Christian love.

The vows have popularly and inadequately been seen as involving sacrificing certain major sources of human fulfilment – possessions, marriage, and independence – the better to answer the call of God. More positive interpretations are current today and given interesting exposition in the literature of the subject. It is claimed that Christian holiness is best seen in terms of loving, of loving liberated from the limitations that continually repress it and restrict its scope. Accordingly, Sister Edna Mary, in *The Religious Life*,[2] discusses the famous vows as the vow of gratitude, the vow of love, and the vow of freedom.

If the vow of poverty is not a negative surrender of the enjoyment of personal possessions but a positive expression of gratitude, it deserves the deepest consideration of every believer.

The principal prayer of the Christian church is the eucharist, a ceremonial and ritual presentation of thankfulness and communion, the essential Christian attitude to experience. Anyone making progress in the Christian life will be finding more in the world to be thankful for and more that he wants to know and love. This will work out in the positive assertion that life is in fact a matter of joy, not things, and that therefore happiness is probably not to be found along the road on which most twentieth-century people are seeking it, which is the acquisition of things.

Moreover, deep within the life of faith there is the strangest of human longings. It has the power to haunt the most unreligious hour. It is the longing to give all to God, to love and serve him with a freedom of movement and width of concern that are unlimited as far as we can make them so. That must be less and less possible the more we are involved in acquiring and managing possessions, investing emotional and financial capital in things.

This desire has nothing whatever to do with any contempt of things in themselves. The world is packed with beautiful and amusing artefacts to delight the imagination and solace anxiety; and the appreciation of them is part of loving God. Wanting to be free to love will involve, however, being alert to the fact that some of life's keenest pleasures and enchanting obsessions, just because of their fascination, can restrict the scope of affection and produce an impoverished life.

Then there is the infinitely darker thing, the world's vast misuse of possessions, a complex of injustice and greed, of triviality and waste, of oppressive deprivation and equally soul-killing abundance. Love's intercession for all who suffer under this terrible weight cannot rest at merely mentioning them in prayer, however devoutly. Such prayer is an uncompleted, abortive thing. Love knows it must do something, not only by political and educational action (which may have to be done by others) but also by some personal renunciation of some part of life's goodness, if not as an act of reparation then as some attempt to alter the balance of our common environment in the direction of a better world.

I believe that any interpretation of Christian spirituality for our day will suggest some such expression of the gratitude and joy that liberate love from preoccupation with things.

The vow of chastity is similarly a form of loving, a vow to love in a specific way. There is a place in the world for the resolve, out of gratitude to God for our nature as lovers, to declare that the essence of love lies in the loving not in the object of the loving. A Christian spirituality would be a working-out of the view that life is for loving, for loving as widely and generously as possible. We are helped to appreciate this by any clear demonstration of loving as an attitude to reality, to reality as a whole and to life as it just comes, rather than as an attachment to one or more chosen objects of love.

Loving as we normally know it is given depth and concentration by selection and preference. Our richest experience of love here and now depends on this, but it is also limited by it.

The Christian imagination is excited by the thought of a universal love, a perfect love like God's. It is to that kind of love that the Lord's prayer is said daily throughout the world. It is that kind of love that will be our life 'tomorrow' when God's will is done on earth as in heaven. In that reconciliation, Jesus said, love is no longer an exclusive thing, as in marrying and giving in marriage, but inclusive and absolute, and no one goes without or is loved less (Luke 20.34–36). There is a call here and now to a kind of loving that suggests this, not choosing and preferring but simply ready to give itself to whomever, to whatever.

There is also the dark side of loving. There is no joy like the joy two lovers can make together, and there is no pain like the pain they can inflict on each other; and there is sometimes only a small space separating that joy and that pain. There is possessive and manipulative love, and love so demanding that there is no room for the loved person at all other than as feeding the lover's egoism; and there is love that is realized only by excluding others from its marvellously private terrain. These distortions and corruptions of love brutalize the emotional life of the world. The call to a love of total welcome and response is a call not only to the fullest expression of our nature as lovers but also to a richness of loving that would be part of our intercession for all whose days are made miseries by love.

The third of the great vows can be seen as revealing the place of obedience in the fullness of freedom. Human beings come to a sense of identity not only through being free to express individual interest and need but also through subjecting their faculty of choice to some purpose that will organize (and therefore necessarily restrict) its energy. There is no identity in sheer freedom, if such a state were possible, only personal disintegration.

In the same way, we need solitude if we are to realize who we are, but we are destroyed by being alone too much. We are made to find fulfilment in companionship with others in a common life.

The political and economic structure of society is a continual change, but whatever love there is in it will imply some good that is recognized by all as good. A society that is merely an aggregate of competing interests is not a society but a chaos. In this country the current tension between government, management and trade unions, with all its difficulties and animosities, is a fascinating example of a community coming to terms with this principle and searching for new and richer forms of corporate life.

Christian obedience to God will be a similar expression of our desire to do the will of God as part of a whole, a universe, rather than as an isolated ego or in the huddle of a few carefully chosen friends of like religious interests.

So, our intercession for the peace of the world is not worth much unless it is completed by the attempt to demonstrate a more excellent way than the self-interest, aggression and defensiveness that ruin human relations everywhere. The church has not been particularly successful in this dimension of holiness, in group spirituality. If it admitted this more honestly than it does, and with more regret, it could then at least humbly claim to know how difficult unity is, as it confronts a divided world. It would also come to a deeper understanding of the mystery that in God's service is perfect freedom. There is no such thing as individual freedom, because no man is an island. Maximum freedom will be the experience of the person whose faculties are functioning at the maximum; and that is not possible without various forms of commitment and responsibility.

Any Christian enquiry into the kind of life that reflects the kingdom of God will find stimulus in this ancient model of the three vows, even though all religious communities today are involved in radical reappraisal of them.

There are not many great ideas of holiness, as there are not many profound elaborations of what love is. It is sensible to explore what we have. Of course, the idea of holiness that grips one generation often dissatisfies the next. Christians are not the only people searching for this bit of truth. Agnostics and humanists who want to know about happiness are really fellow-travellers with them and may well see new aspects of the kingdom or recognize familiar ones more shrewdly than they do. Cyril Connolly, aesthete, critic, intellectual, was once asked what he believed in. He said 'The artist, the saint, the lover, the joker. Them and only them the capitalist cannot buy, the nationalist inflame, or the snob deflate.' It is an engaging comment on the search for the good life. His approved four are all in their different ways people who have achieved some detachment from the world of getting and spending. Theologies and moralities differ and change, but the wisdom of the world has never been in two minds about the place of detachment in a happy life.

In recent years the West has been exposed to non-European cultures as never before. Elements of Asian and African religions and cultures are being absorbed into Western life. This is bound to lead the Christian church to explore new ideas about holiness and reassess old ones. From the same source has come the remarkable widening of compassion, the new concern for the millions in physical want and spiritual deprivation, that has stirred the moral life of the West in our time, particularly among young people. Christian spirituality is bound to be affected by this as new ideals begin to form.

Every period is marked by characteristic failures. Ours today are closely related to the technological advance, economic abundance, erosion of idealism, that have shaped what we are. The main result seems to have been the emergence of personal anxieties and resentments, and the sense of being under pressure, on a scale hitherto unknown.

The light of God's kingdom, if it is to be recognized, must be seen there, in practical compassion for those who suffer from the twentieth century, and in informed concern about the wholeness of personal life.

There is a growing awareness today that the sense of being overburdened and at odds with life has much to do with various kinds of inner division. Our unwillingness to come to terms with what we suppose is the less creditable part of ourselves, our repression of our need for meaning and spiritual hope, our inability to forgive, these together with a chronic reluctance to take responsibility for our own happiness, form only a few of the difficulties that drag down many hundreds of people into depression.

Most of us are ignorant of the inner needs that make us think this, do that, want some other thing. We do not realize how inaccurately we observe ourselves, and other people, when our feelings are keenly disturbing us, or even that we are indeed often so disturbed. A twentieth-century interpretation of the Christian life, of a life in positive relation to the kingdom of God of Jesus' vision, will be less concerned with our generation's outward acts than our fathers were with theirs; it will be much occupied with the inwardness of holiness and with the place of self-understanding in a developing spiritual life.

And forgive us our debts, as we also have forgiven our debtors

EVERY DAY OF his manhood Jesus looked forward, with a hope that seems to have slackened only rarely, to an ultimate joy that would both justify the struggle and waste of things and explain the light that persists in shining in them. He apparently accepted the belief of his tradition that in this joy there would be a 'judgment' of all that had happened in history; that is to say, everything will be seen to have come together into coherent and satisfactory meaning. Most people would like to believe that.

Into this meaning human lives are going to be welcomed. They will find it one of absolute love and understanding, whatever they have done or failed to do. To those who are aware that they deserve something very different from such warmth, that happy culmination of our difficult journey looks like forgiveness. It is the forgiven who eat the bread of life in the happiness of the kingdom. Indeed to eat the bread of life in happiness is what forgiveness is.

That is as true for this world as it is for any next that there may be. To be happy is to be free to welcome life, to be able to go forward into experience trustingly, interestedly, and wanting everyone else to have that kind of freedom and spontaneity.

In comparison with that there is little else that is worth shaping into a prayer. That is actually what we want now, we shall always want it, and maybe most of all for the hour of our death.

Unfortunately, the fullness of that good thing is withheld from most of us.

All our happinesses are diminished by the presence in our minds of a great variety of rages and resentments, against people (for what they have done or ought to have done) and against life itself. These inevitably reduce the welcome we can give to experience, though we may not realize to what extent we are impoverished in this way when life is tolerable enough.

Many people, perhaps not all but certainly most, in occasional moments of truth are disturbed to find that it is much easier for them to take than to give. The sense of their own needs is more real for them than their awareness of other people. You realize that you rarely accord their full value to other lives; you don't grant them their rights; you know that they have rights because you claim to have them too. So there is a heap of ungiven respect, care, love, forbearance you are owing a great number of people.

Certain other details become clear in this not very merciful light – the situations and thoughts you have evaded, usually under the persuasions of vanity or fear, and the sad result of this, the gradual dying of intense emotion because you so often settle for only a fraction of each moment's fullness. It begins to register that you owe something to life itself, you owe it another try. You can do better than the mean and incomplete thing you have made of it. A fresh beginning seems to be required of you, with less of the useless longings that waste life and more genuine joy to dignify it.

Inwardly our resentments and unfulfilled obligations join forces with sinister efficiency and malevolence. Some of the aggression that flows just below the conscious level of the mind, ready to surface at even minor provocation, is really against ourselves, for not meeting the needs of family, friends and acquaintances, who are of course the people who principally represent humanity to us.

This internal malaise is deepened by our sense of life's other unmet requirements, some clear, others just suggested in our vaguer guilts. There is a limit to the amount of this self-dissatisfaction that we can tolerate. We are compelled to divert some of its rancour from ourselves by turning accusingly against life. Inevitably, then, life has to go without still more of the affection we could have given it, would have given it, had our mood been generous.

In some such way, as the years pile up behind us, there accumulates a sense of what we owe to people and to life. It becomes a secret burden. It is often unidentified, but many people have a morose perception of it, keen enough to want to be rid of it, keen enough to guess that some part of them is quietly saying (whether they believe in God or not) 'forgive us our debts, give us to eat the bread of happiness without this humiliating sense of what one owes to the whole blessed show'.

In the Aramaic language, which Jesus spoke, the word used for 'sin' really means a debt; and in Matthew's account of the giving of the Lord's Prayer the word is correctly translated literally with the Greek word for 'debts', though that word is not usually used in Greek for 'sins'.[1]

One of the intriguing things about Jesus was that he seemed to be tired of the way in which conventional piety talked about sin. He had some thoughts of his own on that depressing topic to commend.

It is quite a relief to give the complicated word 'sin' a rest and hear the voice of Jesus in this prayer speaking simply about failure to give oneself where such giving is obviously good, and to see what he saw of the empty world of unmet claims – the love, care, respect not given that should have been given in a thousand encounters.

In the great future to which Jesus looked forward, all these debts will be cancelled by love. A divine freedom of loving and giving will be our element then. He believed that God means us to have some of that freedom of giving now, and so he taught his friends to ask for it now.

Only, on his view, if it is given us, if we do not any longer owe anyone anything, it can only be because we are in fact now giving, and are intending to meet as many of life's claims as we can see.

It is ridiculous to be perfectionist about this. We shall never meet them all, but we can meet some, we can meet more than we have been doing, and we can show willing for the obscure remainder. We begin afresh the life of giving every time we turn to God and receive it from him, every time we enter again into the mind of Jesus and make a bit of it our own.

If ahead of us there is a great forgiveness and reconciliation of life, and loving is going to win in the end, there is a proleptic sense in which everyone can be seen as forgiven and accepted now. That is a very religious idea, typically merciful and dangerous, but not at all outlandish to anyone profoundly affected by Jesus' view that God is for us and his will for us is eternal life.

This vision of the ultimate reconciliation is not merely or even primarily a vision of the future, it is a realization of the deepest 'eternal' character of what it means to be alive in God's world.

For someone to be deeply affected by this understanding of things will mean that he already belongs to it to some extent, is part of it, and is committed to expressing as much of it as can be expressed here and now. He will see that mercy and forgiveness are his route from now on, not rage, or revenge, or sullen non-cooperation.

One of the most dramatic claims on us, which many of us first registered clearly only in the company of Jesus, is that life itself should be forgiven. To adopt Jesus' general spiritual stance, and then to go on being against life, accusing it under one's breath as a misguided, unjust affair, would mean to have misunderstood Jesus completely. If he is right, we, in such a mood, cannot possibly be right.

When things go wrong for us we prefer to take angry and condemnatory views, accusing life of owing us this and that. If we are able to achieve some relaxation and detachment, another truth alights upon the mind, like a fluttering herald of peace, that if we cannot just now see life as good we can certainly see that it needs help, is in some sense wounded, and part of us at any rate wants to help it. When we think that way it is clear that we have received forgiveness, however it came, because we ourselves are forgiving.

In Jesus' sharp, logical mind, forgiveness is always known in our forgivingness. That is the only way in which it can be known, that is to say, in our giving up a considerable range of claims and expectations – for example, for some kind of compensatory return after injury, indeed for payment of anything thought to be our due.

It is easy to see when in this way our style changes from getting, or wanting, to giving. When with his help it happened to a woman Jesus knew, she was so excited at the new feel of life that she went looking for him, tracked him down at a famous dinner party (where she was certainly not expected), and, to the surprise of all and the irritation of some, thanked him with extravagant grace. In the argument that ensued Jesus pointed out that you could easily tell that it had happened to her, that she had come to see life as God's love and herself as no longer owing him a single thing (whatever the world said about her), because there was so much love in her, pushing her into giving.

She is a tantalizingly obscure creature in the story (Mark 14.3–9); and there is much we want to know about her and never shall. She may have been quite unexceptional, one of society's small-scale characters in whose lives there is little to hide and less to be proud of; but there was this one quick moment, perhaps the first genuine act of choice in a life determined by others. In it what forgiveness means flashed before a very ordinary world in an instant of brightness.

Something like that woman's specific sense of an entirely new feeling about life can be seen as the initial excitement in which the Christian church began its chequered life. Since the friends of Jesus abandoned him when he was arrested, and disintegrated in terror, how did the Christian church get going at all? C. H. Dodd suggested that it was not just the inspiration of the resurrection.[2] That this frightened and ashamed group had a mysterious experience of Jesus returning to them with the look of a man who has done the impossible and come through death would simply have intensified their guilt with the mind-chilling aura of the supernatural they now saw about their friend whom they had so disgracefully abused. The decisive feature of the experience was not just that it was one of Jesus in some way returning to them after death; it was that this extraordinary event was an experience of forgiveness.

The crucial scene is described in John 21.15–19. The risen Jesus, with a precise thoroughness of affection, covers all Peter's denials with simple persuasions to him to trust the love he is sure he feels, and with assurances that he is in fact free to express his love and can now go forward.

That scene, which constituted Peter's re-instatement as 'a Christian' and gave him a fresh start, has definitive significance for the origin and essence of the Christian church. Certainly it is right for it to understand itself as the community of the resurrection; but much more, and more importantly, it is the community of the forgiven. Naturally then, it will come to see itself, however challenging this insight will repeatedly be in years to come, as the community of the forgiving.

It is a beautiful idea. It is also a terror to the conscience to be committed to something so appealing and yet so difficult. There is little evidence that Christians, as a church or as individuals, are particularly good at forgiving.

It is a dark fact which they are never allowed to forget; and it is part of their pain that somehow they have to learn to live with it.

Whenever they read the account of Jesus teaching his friends to pray, they see once again that, according to him, being forgiven is so tied to forgiving that he had to underline it with some seriousness, as though the rest of the prayer could take its chance in their minds but that particular point was one they really must get right (Matt. 6.14; cf. Mark 11.25).

Whenever they say the Apostles' Creed they say that they do indeed believe in the forgiveness of sins. That does not mean just that we hold the opinion that God forgives sins, but that we believe that forgiving sins is one of the constitutive principles of life, God's life and man's life, however disappointed the world may be at seeing so little sign of this.

And they make quite an issue of it at every eucharist. In the eucharist, before the bread and wine are offered, gifts of the earth and the work of human hands, to become knowledge and love of the creator of everything, the worshippers greet one another in the happy solemnity of the peace. It is happy because it is a moment of freedom to be friends; the joy of it is best seen in a student congregation. It is serious because behind it is one of the characteristically searching requests of Jesus:

If you are offering your gift at the altar, and there remember that your brother has something against you, leave your gift there before the altar and go; first be reconciled to your brother, and then come and offer your gift (Matt. 5.23f.).

We make a gesture of general reconciliation. It may be a mile away from love, but it is a step, it is a confession that we do wish to go there, and it is certainly kinder than no gesture at all. It can take as much meaning as anyone cares to give it. It symbolizes forgiveness both sought and given, because what 'your brother' has against you may well be that you have not yet forgiven him.

After this, the hand that has been offered with the peace of God, in the peace of God, to my neighbour (who ritually stands for everyone I know and indeed all the world) can rightly be stretched out to take the bread of God's mercy and the wine of life.

The eucharist and the Lord's Prayer carry as much meaning and emotion as we can give to our praying at the time. We are often disappointed at the amount we can give. Sometimes, no doubt, the substance of the peace is meagre in the extreme, something 'simple and faithless as a smile and shake of the hand'. That does not prevent it being haunted by what it might mean.

It may be that the reluctance in many churches to make anything of it is a sign in itself, is really a shrinking from the approach and appeal of love, the love that is always hovering somewhere in Christ's religion.

There is more, however, in these religious occasions than the meaning we bring to them. They have a power of presence in themselves, independently of any life we give or fail to give them. To use them is to renew the bond between us and spiritual realities deeper and more faithful than our very moderate spiritual efforts. Seven times out of ten we sense them again in this way, simply by placing ourselves back in a traditional Christian setting. Occasionally their impact is exceptionally strong.

There are times when you are able truly to respond to the *Sursum corda*, when you do succeed in lifting up your heart into the world of thankfulness and offering that the eucharist is; and then you are astonished to find that you can indeed forgive every injury you have ever suffered, have done so now (however quickly on leaving the church you resume your smaller mind), and feel that you are never going to die. These good moments are not easily erased from the mind. Sometimes you find yourself surviving on the memory of them.

It has to be admitted that there are some situations of malevolence in which it is hard to see what room there is for God, though of course he must be present in some odd disguise or other. The other day a happy and attractive small boy, doing his morning paper round, was murdered. How can his parents think compassionately about the man who murdered their son? Never, without God. Yet there does not seem to be much hope for us unless they can manage it. Their fury must increase unless they, their son, his attacker, are called into some new kind of life in which people look mercifully at one another, refreshed by understanding. Glimpses of such a life come. The trouble is that they vanish too. It sometimes seems that a thousand eucharists, a thousand Our Fathers have left us much as we were.

That fact of life is upsetting only if you hold superficial views of progress. Does anything improve as the years leave us and go

God knows where? Obviously here and there particular sets of circumstances improve, though not necessarily finally, since they may deteriorate and need repair. Still, it is obvious that many kinds of knowledge grow from more to more, and there is much knowledge that is not easily lost.

It is all very different in the matter of understanding the tremendous life inside oneself and coping with its lonely fires and anxieties and its questions as to what one is actually for. Each of us has to do that for himself, as though it has never been done before, and again and again, since the mind frequently interprets experience mistakenly, and often forgets.

And this work of interpretation is apt to be much in arrears. Life's joys and griefs leave behind a trail of knowledge in the mind which many of us never begin to follow until it is almost too late. Even if we are lucky enough to get some of the work done in reasonable time, no insight is ever gained once and for all. We live from day to day – in a sense, as both eucharist and Lord's Prayer suggest – from hand to mouth, looking to God for what turns life into praise.

What matters is that as a result of the hundreds of eucharists, Lord's Prayers, and many other experiences mulled over as best you can, you come to understand what it means to live life in the light cast on it by Jesus, and to live it with the new shadow you are trailing now you are in his light.

It certainly means to be able to live with your failures without despairing. You can tolerate the left-behind feeling that comes from seeing how often you go backwards when most other people appear able to go on, because the important thing is that here, where you are, is God. He still walks with us, and most of all when someone we have offended moves off with a superior gait.

Then there is, surely, a warmer attitude to others. If this does not happen, we may succeed in stopping feeling guilty but we have not been given forgiveness. Jesus was so emphatic about this in his comment on the prayer he taught his friends that anyone who thinks he has received forgiveness without becoming more clear about God's will for him, without feeling a new desire to do it, without a fresh openness to the world (especially the world as dispenser of hurts) has not received what Jesus understood by forgiveness.

I believe that one of the ways in which a warmer attitude to others grows in us is through understanding the hold of the past in people's lives, and being very sympathetic about that.

It is only our insignificant and trivial experiences that are simply lived through, to vanish without remainder. Those that carry considerable emotional discharge, like loves and losses, seem to cling to us and dog our footsteps. Whatever may be the truth about the sway of original sin in our lives, there is certainly an original wound in many lives from which the victims never recover, though some are able to give it a positive role. At the back of many people's minds is the thought of some experience they hope will never happen again, some delight they long to recover, or some missed part of life's goodness they wish they had had.

These ghosts of our mental life increase the difficulty of self-understanding, which is not easy even on our most lucid days, other souls being so often, so it seems, clear to us, our own so frequently hidden in some perverse mist. You may think that the need for comfort or encouragement that is bothering you today is to be referred to some recent irritation or humiliation, but its root may go a long way down. It could be drawing its nuisance value from some reverse in your very early days. In his poem 'Germinal' the poet known as 'A.E.' wrote:

In ancient shadows and twilights
Where childhood had strayed,
The word's great sorrows were born
And its heroes were made.
In the lost boyhood of Judas
Christ was betrayed.[3]

This long-distance influence of the past can sometimes be identified in our periodic over-reactions to experience, when we realize that our emotional response to a situation is really in excess of the facts; but it is a difficult area of life, most of us having on our hands considerable unfinished business with our past. It is part of loving our neighbour as ourself to see that this is how it is with him too.

There is a prayer that asks Christ to stand behind us to defend us from the assaults of the past. Yet that does not seem to be quite the way he works with the past. If the past is given to him, he takes it, blesses it, changes its substance and makes it an acceptable presence, something we no longer need to fear or rage about but can take into ourselves as life, goodness of life.

That is a religious and sacramental way of putting something that involves plenty of work.

Jesus said that there are some inner furies that can be cast out only by prayer and fasting, that is to say, by meditation and some disciplined strategy to help the self to grow and come to maturity (Matt. 17–21).

The meditation will be the sort that helps us to live in the present, evaluating it directly, not getting it wrong because of the distorting influence of the past. This will mean some working through our depressions and angers, realizing how much emotional hangover from spent situations in the past is in them, and reshaping our wants in terms of what is now possible.

Fasting, as essentially doing without, could be interpreted for today as the effort to jettison certain feelings, for example, habitual longings and grievances, that are no use at all in the current situation – indeed are a nuisance in that they prevent one participating in life's enjoyments.

It is good to have in our life, for whatever reason, some attempt to go without this or that, as a kind of raid on our demand for compensations of various kinds, as a reduction of the amount of emotional indulgence in our daily diet.

It also gives our capacity for making an effort some practice. That capacity is an early casualty when life goes wrong for us. In its place comes boredom, the vague sense of all the unlived life one has within and that there is nothing now to be done about it. Boredom is the principal monitory signal of the onset of despair.

The reflective effort to see things more clearly is fortunately not the extent of what can be done in our difficulties. Small gestures of interest towards other people, bits of ordinary human pleasing and consoling, work an incidental grace of widening our own imaginations. They are not done for that reason of course, though no good is ever done purely disinterestedly. In the general mix of life, the capacity for sympathy to be seen in some people who have been much hurt by experience has often been roused actually by their being hurt. They know now how painful pain can be.

It is often the case that the healing of a woe has not come from receiving the sympathy of another person but largely through giving sympathy to another. Our power to give and forgive, to bear and forbear, is often excited and made available to us by compassionate contact with someone else's need to receive grace. To be concerned with someone else and mix his hurt or need or happiness with our angry or sad preoccupations actually dilutes them and saves them from being the lethal draught they tend to be in our solitude.

It is a very sensible meditation to reflect that the other people in our lives, from whom we secretly expect the replenishing of what is missing in ours, are all walking in their private version of emotional scarcity just as much as we are. In such a world, to try to cultivate some small skill to please and amuse and assist looks like one of the more intelligent purposes. The modesty of this proposal is part of its realism. So often the big gesture is just not required; the crumbs of beauty one must have to be able to continue are comparatively few.

To have something to forgive represents quite a programme. In any reflecting on a hurt, somewhere near the beginning one needs to ask what exactly can be done about it. The conventional hope is in the external solution, in some change in the offender altering everything for the better, with the resentment dispelled by the offender's acknowledgment, regret, apology and resolve not to offend again. Sometimes this happens, but not always; and sometimes it happens to such little effect in the wounded heart that it is a question what exactly it amounts to, since it is clear that something else has to happen to bring release there.

It is the release in the wounded heart that matters. When that release comes it often so changes the sufferer's attitude to the offender that his acknowledgment and apology become secondary affairs, whether they have or have not yet occurred.

That is the true release, because it is the point of growth in the whole situation. The true release is not when a state of tension and grievance is brought to an end. It is when the conflict situation is transformed into one of new possibility so that it becomes a new beginning.

Time spent in thinking about this inwardness of forgiveness

is one of the better ways of spending time. Forgiveness is a programme of work you have to do on yourself. It is a blessing that, primarily at any rate, does not reside in any change in the other person, in some contrite act on his part.

In domestic conflict, for example, there has often been such an accumulation of secret woe through the years that neither side is really free to acknowledge fault.

What is possible, though of course never easy, is the transferring of attention from the other person's inadequacy to one's own resentment, fear, demands. When these are seen, if only moderately clearly, and so have become able to sustain at least some scrutiny, they lose some of their inevitability. They begin to be to some extent accepted. They become part of oneself in its freedom, instead of part of oneself in its blind compulsiveness.

In this inner loosening and acceptance, even if in only one of the disputants, the total situation changes, and the relationship does now begin to move. Life begins again in it.

And it is the only way in which this can happen. Apology and acceptance, forgive and forget, are of use only in the most superficial tensions, where a pact that can be concluded in half a minute has perhaps some relevance. Where the hurt is deep, and emotional blood is flowing, apology by itself can be part of love's dying, not its resurrection. The fact is that each of the unhappy pair has now work to do, and what matters is whether they are going to set about it.

Those who know most about forgiving know that it is not the operation of some forgive and forget principle but a depth of loving that includes compassionate remembering. Just as my own rages and dreads are part of me, what my friend has done or said that has thrown our love into fiendish disarray is part of him. It may seem to me quite uncharacteristic and inexplicable, or I may recognize it as a reaction to some inner dismay of his with which all who know him are familiar. In either case, at its root is some need or fear that is part of his being.

Loving, if it is the genuine article, acknowledges that, is tender to it, accepts it as part of the truth to be lived with, and without grievance or despair lives out its open-ended faith in what being loved may at length bring to him.

When it is we ourselves who are in the wrong and in one way or another want to find the arms of life around us again, the spirituality of the situation has much to do with negotiating the feeling of guilt.

People cannot go on day after day feeling sorry for what they have done. If they try, they only make themselves ill and can indeed in this way destroy every bit of good in them.

Guilt-feeling is one of God's most dangerous gifts. Still, there is no doubt that it is a gift, part of the goodness of life. The positive use in it is that unless we feel, in a gutsy way, what it is to be in the wrong we shall register this only with our brains. Our brains are so clever at evasion and rationalization that we may understand what we have done quite inadequately. You can play around with self-justifications and special pleadings until you end up lost in a fog of lies.

The function of this deep feeling is to act as an alarm signal. Just as the purpose of fear is to announce danger and stimulate appropriate action, that of guilt is similarly protective, to announce wrongness and stimulate appropriate action.

The suitable action is a three-stage affair involving the accurate appraisal of the situation, the discernment of the present possibilities of restoring it to rightness or bringing some kind of good out of it, and the assumption of whatever responsibility for this good future I am able to carry.

It is only as a stimulus to this programme of action that guilt-feeling and regretful sorrow are any use at all. They may operate still at stage one, but if they operate too intensely there, they will obscure the facts to be acknowledged. It is best if the first stage is as brief as possible and we soon turn our attention to the rest of the action to be taken. It may be that regret for the past may continue to provide some fuel for this action, but it will be a very subsidiary element in the process. Hopefulness and confidence and interest in the future are the best suppliers of energy now.

Unfortunately, this good gift of God, the sense of life's wrongness, often functions destructively in many of us, and sometimes in all of us. It is often a liability in people whose religious and moral education has been narrow and prejudiced, who are goaded by mistaken ideals, or have had too early some experience of being sent outside the feast of life. In them too sharp an awareness of exclusion is at work, and a persisting sense of never doing anything properly. Their conscience gives them a terrible time.

Yet we have no need to take the messages of our conscience at their face value. My conscience is not some infallible faculty of discernment that tells me what I should do and what my moral grading is.

My conscience is my mind when it is making moral judgments, when it is occupied in the sometimes very tricky estimating of what is right and what is wrong in a proposed course of action. It is not by any means always reliable.

It is not uncommon for conscience to be tyrannical, and ignorant with it, persecuting people with feelings of guilt over stupid things, and stunting their growth with an accumulated sense of failure.

That sort of conscience is no gift of God. It is not the working of our adult moral being but a hangover from childhood. It is the persisting small child in us, frightened of losing parental

78

love, of not measuring up to parental requirements (some of which may have been quite mistaken). As we grow older, this parental love that we fear to lose merges with our adult social environment, our world of work, family and friends, so that the requirements of that world now provoke anxiety and we fear to lose its support and regard.

The result in the extreme case is a life of misery, in the same way in which life is a misery for a child of narrow, over-strict parents who nag endlessly and plant in their offspring the compulsion to please and an equally compulsive tendency to feel hurt and to be driven into self-contempt.

This obsessional conscience is little use in the adult life of moral growth. It is good for us all when it is challenged, though that challenge is heard more often in the world of the novel and the theatre than in the Christian church. Not that it matters where God's word of life is spoken as long as it gets spoken.

The sense of the gap between us and God is related often to childhood experience and early religious instruction that have burned deep into the mind (the scar may be there for ever) the conviction that God likes us only if and when we behave well, as perhaps, rightly or wrongly, we got the impression that our parents only really liked us if and when we behaved well.

The penitence that results from this mouldy version of the gospel is little more than self-contempt and depression, and about as much use. A climate of failure prevails, and the little regulations by which one attempts to keep one's life in some kind of order provide about as much help as sandbags in a swollen tide. It was precisely against that dreadful kind of religion that the voice of Jesus was raised as he walked among us in his vision of a better life.

It would be a relief for many people if they followed him

and breathed the fresh and hopeful air of his spiritual mind. God loves us as we are. It is not the case that we are accepted only as we measure up to the stature of the fullness of Christ, nor even if that impossible condition is qualified into 'when we are "in Christ" ', justified by faith, or some other evangelical subtlety that can leave people as perplexed as ever. Human sin is in the nature of things, like the tears Virgil's mind was continually hearing. Jesus wished to assure people of all kinds, and especially those who were having a difficult and helpless time with themselves, that God loved them, and as much when they were heading for sin as when they were managing a spell of virtue.

All of us wish to love life and other people, and to be on better terms with our own personality, stuck as we are with it for better or worse. When things go wrong, our awareness of that is a providential sign that some work is to be done. If it merely divides one into two partial selves, one cursing the other, there is about as much hope and grace in that as there is in a tantrum. What is happening then is that a God-given function, of considerable delicacy, is being misused. Much more sensible, indeed the way forward, is to question the assumptions we have been making about what matters in life, to ask what mistaken prides and hopes have been keeping us going, and whether there is better fuel available.

This recognition of necessary changes in one's aims and expectations is a highly important part of any sane idea of forgiveness. When it is managed successfully it is a hopeful and constructive experience. To follow such questions deeply into oneself produces a kind of honest peace; peace, because it is seen that in this world responsibility for wrong is infinitely shared, and so the sense of wrong is not allowed to be infinitely, and so unbearably, subjective; honest, because we know that we have co-operated in the making of life's evil. Part of what has gone wrong is our fault, and even the part we need not so summarily shoulder is not remote enough to be easily dismissed from our concern. We may be victims of this or that person's malevolence, but there is a kind of inner collaboration between us and our persecutors through that in us, or that lack in us, that provoked them. However much you rage against things, from among its million disagreeable faces life can always turn towards you one that is your own.

The Christian church sees an intimate connection between the cross of Jesus and forgiveness. When we say that 'Christ died for our sins', to bring us forgiveness, it is a Christian way of saying that he lived and died, loved and taught, to bring us the certainty of God's unending love which no sin can ever interrupt.

The choice of his death rather than his life as the dominant image of this is due to the fact that his death completed his commitment to his task in the most dramatic and convincing way open to man, since he could have avoided his death by surrendering his task.

The moment of his death was the moment of his finished work in that until that moment it was still possible for him to abandon God and us. That is why his death has all the way through haunted, almost obsessed, the Christian imagination as the supreme focus and validation of that truth about God he was continually offering the world.

Whatever the future of the church of his name, he must remain for thousands the embodiment of what they long to hear about life. Whatever good there is in Christianity, he himself is its central glory and makes all the rest of it nothing more than a cloudy rim.

Any utterance about what is thought to be God must be

incomplete, complex in meaning, and necessarily involve images which both demand and defy explanation because they are rooted in the unconscious depths of our minds. To many people it is an important part of the appeal of Jesus that he spoke in an approximate, inexact way, using a kind of groping and evocative style, presenting his hearers with situations and conclusions that disturbed and excited them but, so it seems, with the limited purpose of giving them just some idea of what it could mean to trust God – it's like this, it's like that, the kingdom of God is like so and so.

All these images together do not make a straightforward and clear theology. They obviously disturbed and confused people's minds, yet at the same time strongly suggested a better world than this one (with which, incidentally, he seems to have found it difficult to conceal his impatience), a world that had an exciting appeal but a trustworthy appeal because there was something so convincingly genuine about the speaker. Every generation since seems to have been delighted with the report that he impressed people not just as someone usually clever and at home with a lot of deep ideas, but as one who spoke with the power of a man who knew what he was talking about.

What he was will always elude our descriptions, but no one reading what he is understood to have taught can avoid concluding that he had an extraordinary mental *rapport* with people who were plagued by the sense of wrongness, in themselves and in life. This peculiar obsession with the disappointed, the failed, the victim receives an additional, indirect emphasis from his obvious reservations about success and comfort and the whole dingy fashionable world of the successful and comfortable. Certainly much of the time he appears to be addressing people who know what it is to be disappointed with themselves.

What he offered them was comforting but it was not a facile

comfort. It was not the 'it isn't as bad as you think' tranquillizer. Sometimes it is much worse than we think. He simply assured them that underneath everything, however great the tangle, however indefensible we are, we are not in the very least cut off from God and his love. In this respect sin and virtue are almost irrelevant, just as success and failure, being in a mess or emerging from one are irrelevant. Whatever the conditions, the moment we want God we have him. That moment we are with him and he with us.

In this notably forward-looking attitude, blame seems to have hardly any place. On more than one occasion Jesus made it clear how uneasy he was in the world of fault-finding. He gives the impression that he thought that responsibility for evil, both general and particular, is a highly complex and mysterious realm, and that human beings have not the brains to cast up the accounts there with anything like accuracy.

When anyone's life goes wrong, and he feels it to be wrong, the responsibility that matters is that of doing what is possible to help it to come right, and being willing to accept God's present help in the pains and difficulties that usually accompany things coming right. Having God in the wrongness of things is one and the same as being caught up in the thrust and energy of his working to help them come right. The two sides of forgiveness belong together with an absolutely logical inevitability that makes either side by itself as unreal as a dream, or a nightmare. To separate them is to destroy the whole idea.

That God is never anything but love is a useless conviction to anyone who does not wish to be caught up in his purpose. That God's forgiveness is the beginning of a considerable programme of work on ourselves and our predicaments may well be unbearable unless we are certain that he is with us to love and guide us through to a better way of being ourselves.

Most people seem to have to work things out alone. None should resign themselves to that isolation without first looking round to see what help is available. The Christian life is too difficult, and religious experience is too susceptible to illusion and mistake, to be pursued alone, but no more I suppose than any other attempt to live by some spiritual aim or ideal. Human beings need each other. In the Genesis story, the fruit of the tree of knowledge was good to eat for that reason. The eyes of them both were opened and they knew they were naked. It produced this moment of realization how defenceless and unprotected men and women are, and that they need one another to survive.

When life goes wrong it is as likely as not to be some mistaken aims that are sending it awry, rather than some failure to reach obvious good. There is a strong probability that we shall more than occasionally aim at the wrong things if we refer only to ourselves, instead of to the innumerable sufferings and learnings of the past, and to the wisdom and skill available in our own time. Many people are at work to reconcile troubled lives and life, counsellors, priests, doctors, though it is frequently said (Jesus was the first to make the point) that such good workers in the fields of human anxiety are desperately few for the harvest of insight and compassion that can be gathered there to revive and sustain the life of the world.

And lead us not into temptation, but deliver us from evil

IN FRANZ KAFKA'S NOVEL *The Castle*,[1] a man has been given the work of agent in a village for the authorities at the castle near by. He wants to find out what his duties are, but he has great difficulty in getting into touch with these authorities, so much so that he begins to wonder exasperatingly not only who they are but whether they exist at all and whether his job is not some quite mistaken notion. I sometimes think we are similarly tantalized when we think of Jesus.

There are times when the way in which he experienced life and the style in which he communicated his vivid experience seem quite clear. Fifty years ago preachers used to speak of Jesus with genuine warmth and affection as the most knowable person in the world, but not now.

In all remembering, fact and fantasy merge and separate and combine again in indistinguishable waves. The Christian image of Jesus, its mixture of historical recall and religious experience, comes dim and clear by turns in our changeable intellectual weather. It is as if we keep losing and finding a loved companion in a mountain mist and begin to wonder if it is indeed always our friend who every so often appears as the wind and cloud recede.

His presence is much larger in our lives than the figure in the pages of the New Testament, and it seems to press harder in what goes on in your mind after you have read his words than in the words themselves. Yet you cannot help wanting to make the difficult, perhaps fruitless, journey back into the past to find this man to whom life brought his unique vocatoin, with its caring and not caring, whose friends then and since have felt he was the only sane person in the world.

The older one grows and the more one thinks about him the more mysterious he seems, but he is never dull. Life comes to us most of the time in small bits, and it is easy to be bored. With him there seems a great fund of surprise and sense of novelty. You feel that had he lived longer he would always have looked at the world, even until old age, with the eyes of a child and of a revolutionary by turns. And yet, if there were no miracle stories (inconvenient as they are to the rational mind) would we in fact think of the Jesus of the New Testament as a particularly compassionate man?

Then there are his severe strictures against being anxious, the blithe calls for trust. He seems to have lived a Bohemian kind of life, in the sense that it appears to have been a wandering existence, no house, no home, no two days alike, waking up in the morning not knowing where you would sleep that night, not caring perhaps.

Speculations like these still turn the eyes of the restless, young and old, in his direction. Though they are only speculations, his life was certainly nothing like ours, diverted by a bus or train to catch each morning, children to educate, bills flicking chirpily through the letterbox on the first of each month. These differences inevitably distance him from us, along with the more private strains that divide everyone from everyone else.

Generations have seen in him an innocent victim of some

vast circumstance involving us all, whether or not we wish to be drawn into its mystery. You wonder how much of that touched his heart; and you end by consigning it to all that about him into which we just can't enter, for lack of imagination and for lack of love.

He was certainly a man with the world against him, and huddling down for a bit of warmth in the friendship of twelve men who were not particularly dependable but do seem to have helped him.

Yet the man who looks at you from the pages of the New Testament is not a frightened creature. As a human being he obviously needed to be afraid and react suitably when threatened. Otherwise, like the rest of us, he wouldn't have lasted a day; but this good instinct never became a crack in his selfhood through which his enthusiasm leaked away. He was always having a real go at life, whether it took the shape of a storm at sea or the looming figure of 'that fox' Herod.

There was, however, one unusual fear, all along the secret sharer of his thoughts, that one needs to understand if one is going to understand him.

His mind had been formed in a spiritual tradition that had jettisoned all expectations that human beings, with or without the help of God, would bring about a perfectly satisfactory world. In place of that old utopian dream the dominant idea now was that such fulfilment was indeed to come but it would come as a result of the merciful action of God. From the divine compassion, and from nowhere else, would come the new age of joy in life and in God, of universal love and peace, of forgiveness and spiritual power.

One sinister theme, however, darkened this bright expectation. There was general agreement that shortly before the great day came there would be its dark herald. This would be a time of unprecedented testing, of unnatural happenings, persecutions, pseudo-prophets and false saviours, and such confusion of values that even the light of truth would be held by the hand of doubt.

This terrible last effort on the part of evil would test people's faith in God as nothing before and surely find out those who did and those who did not hold to God through good and ill and trust in his unfailing love and so be worthy of the new age.

It was called The Temptation, the great trial.

It was that threat, all the darker because he saw it against the blaze of light behind it that was God's promised new world and life, that was the shadow of the kingdom in the mind of Jesus, and led him to conclude the prayer he taught his friends with 'and lead us not into temptation, but deliver us from evil'.

The whole prayer is affected by this. All its askings take on some of the dye of fear in which the end of it has been dipped.

Jesus tells his friends to ask for nothing less than the ultimate good that most human hearts have caught themselves wanting at some time or other, the absolute that is beyond tomorrow, with its universal hallowing of God's name by forgiven and satisfied beings doing his will on a new earth where nothing goes wrong. They are to ask for this, the seemingly impossible best, because it has already begun to appear in the life and work of Jesus. He is the guarantee that it is coming and that it will not be long now.

He made it clear, however, that their entry into this tremendous happiness is profoundly linked to their living as far as they can here and now by the light of what he told them about it. And precisely there, at that point, the believer's heart begins to fear.

He cannot help it. We do not do so well at living by the values of the kingdom of heaven even now, in the normal strains and stresses. How we shall fare in the Great Temptation, or that particularly searching pressure which the expression may serve to symbolize in our case, must always be uncertain.

However strange this part of the mind of Jesus may seem to us, it is just the case that by the Temptation, the Test, the Trial (whatever word is used in the most inconvenient proliferation of versions of the Lord's Prayer in our time), is not meant the ordinary testings or everyday life.

They are certainly testings and it is absurd to be casual about them. Under them our shaky emotional structure, sometimes held together by little more than unsatisfactory rivets of resentment and fear, often creaks and gives way. Still, it does not always give way, because in every life there are challenges that with the help of some grace are met and turned to good account and so add to the momentum of one's confidence.

Everyone knows that the resistance of things excites effort in us and that it is by meeting difficulty, and indeed also through failure to meet it, that we learn the better and worse ways of picking our route through experience.

In the Bible there is a quite positive attitude to this. It is seen as part of the goodness of life that we are tempted, that our resolution and convictions are put to the test in various ways. As Christian spirituality began to form and elaborate in the life and teaching of the early fathers, there was a shrewd appreciation of it. There is a pleasant example quoted by Thomas Merton in *The Wisdom of the Desert*:

Abbot Pastor said that Abbot John the Dwarf had prayed to the Lord and the Lord had taken away all his passions, so that he became impossible. And in this condition he went to one of the elders and said: You see before you a man who is completely at rest and has no more temptations. The elder said: Go and pray to the Lord to command some struggle to be stirred up in you, for the soul is matured only in battles. And when the temptations started up again, he did not pray that the struggle be taken away from him, but only said: Lord, give me strength to get through the fight.[2]

So, to pray 'lead us not into temptation' cannot mean to ask for exemption from the normal opportunities of failure and success through which an adult self is made. That would amount to not wanting to live. What the prayer has in view is this last extraordinary test, with its persecutions and bewilderments, that Jesus believed would herald the fulfilment of God's promise to give his creation the absolute joy.

That being so, it could not have made sense to pray literally that we should not be led into it. It is coming. No prayer is going to save us from that special fight. Actually there is no problem. It is now generally understood that the expression 'lead us not into' refers not to meeting the trial but to breaking under it, to succumbing to one form or another of the evil ahead in the last dreadful days.[3]

There must be many people who cannot follow Jesus the whole distance and detail of this vision of the future. They do not have this sense of an imminent end of things heightening every tension and every pleasure. They may well agree that not all moments are the same, that for many people there is one they particularly await, with longing or fear. Apart from that, the more common feeling is that the days slip by and seem to touch very little as they pass, and there is not much chance of one's contributing much to the totality of the world's affairs. Perhaps it is lack of alertness and imagination that makes them interpret the signals of experience in such a pedestrian way.

Jesus was quick to read this situation. He caught people's

mood and sensed what their words implied of the negative momentum their lives had acquired. He noted the faces that no longer had that expression of pleasant anticipation of what life has to offer that is to be seen in the very young and sometimes appears again with a deeper light in the very old. It troubled him.

His concern is behind all that he said about people missing life's goodness by being too late in one sense or another, or too nervous to risk a fall, or too preoccupied substituting minor gratifications for substantial ones.

And he often made use of his dramatic sense of time as virtually throbbing with imminent happening. Because he was continually alert to the new day which he believed was even now breaking on the long night of human life, that awareness became a kind of conceptual model by which he interpreted one human experience after another.

However dead you may feel, this very moment is one in which God's voice may call you out of your tomb, and you can begin again, maybe with less comfort because less self-deception, but full of hope. And all the smaller tests of life he interpreted as foreshadowings of the coming great trial (sometimes it seems almost the trial itself) since matters of the greatest moment may be decided in them. When Jesus recommends quick agreement with your accuser lest you lose your case altogether and suffer the extreme penalty, it may be just a specimen of oriental prudential wisdom, but there is a dark eschatological hint in the tone of it that suggests the seriousness of final things. Sometimes it is only this that saves our attention from wandering; the story of the wise and foolish virgins would seem to us an archaic bore were it not for the edge of terror just beneath its surface.

In happier vein, in his meals with his friends, with shady tax-officials and other disreputable types, with crowds come to hear his teaching, it seems that the thought of the feast beyond to-morrow was often nudging his mind and giving him the sense that this occasion, whatever its apparent character, was even now invested with that ultimate reality, much as the church later came to see the sacraments as not only symbols and re-minders but actual carriers of the divine presence, real comings of the kingdom of heaven.

Similarly, our deliverances from evil, our multitudinous awareness of life's fascination and pleasure, are good in them-selves, and in this Christians and humanists stand happily together; but there is another dimension to the experience, not credible to the humanist, which gives all earthly beauty a special radiance for Christians as an anticipation of the fantastic happiness awaiting the world, indeed as a true bearer and beginning of it.

This heightened awareness that charges every moment with marvellous and dreadful potentiality is one of Jesus' charac-teristic gifts to the spirit of man. To live with such a keen sense of how much things matter, how much is to be lost or gained, would result in an extremely tense and strained kind of life unless a delicate balance is found between fear and the expecta-tion of deliverance.

We know that we are free to fail, and that sometimes we shall; we know that we could lose all along the line, and finally lose the kingdom. We also know that the kingdom of God is forgiveness and new life, and that its welcoming door is open-ing to us all the time we are turning into or drifting down the mistaken path. The only way of maintaining these two spiritual facts at their full value is in some uneasy prayer like 'help us not to yield when our faithfulness is tested, and bring us through every encounter with evil'.

There has always been this unease in the Christian way. No

one has offered to remove it, outside the ludicrous confidence of sectarian pietism. As a matter of fact, Christian spirituality has made extensive use of the dilemma. It gives the screw of difficulty just another turn and tells us that we would be fools not to feel this uncertainty and equally foolish to succumb to it. From the solemn giving of the Lord's Prayer to this day Christian's have been continually warned against two extremes in our anxiety over whether we shall or shall not get through; one is presumption, the other is despair.

So, if this prayer is not allowed to become a dead repetition but is thoroughly worked into one's life, it will involve finding some way of living with the fear of evil, with our awareness that much can go wrong with the world and much can go wrong with oneself.

We are never going to have any success in negotiating this fear unless there is room in our minds for the fact that there is much that actually goes right in this world.

It is worth while being on the look-out for life's tendency to contract under pressure, and sometimes for no positive reason at all other than boredom and inertia. The imagination needs variety of experience just as the body needs a certain variety of foods. Alongside the mind's ability to respond in terror to things, there needs to be cultivated its equally definite but not always so robust ability to delight in life, to indulge curiosity and admiration, to be interested and amused.

It is likely that the more you see the calmer you are. Fearing is often connected with some form of mental claustrophobia. Unless there is some deliberate attempt to savour and collect the enjoyable things with which God surrounds human anxiety, the day-to-day accumulation of minor guilts, small losses and worries easily inflates into overwhelming woe, and before long you are waking most mornings with the suspicion that life's raised whip is sure to descend on you again today. The strain of this reduced world is soon unbearable. One longs for a holiday from oneself; and there is no such thing. No one can take you out of yourself.

Another person may surmise, perhaps suggest, what the ache in my heart may mean or what decisions may reduce it, but only I can extend the range of things I think about. Unless I am truly obsessionally ill, I am free to do this. It is sensible to do it. It is part of that due concern for oneself that Jesus had in mind when he commented so sadly about people gaining the whole world and losing the most precious thing of all, losing one's responding and affectionate self. The more one sees of, enjoys being involved in, is intrigued by, the human condition, the less one fears evil.

Then when evil actually confronts us, it confronts beings who know some other things about life, its many varieties of goodness, its endless movement and hopefulness, and other features of it that our journey through pleasure and pain has commended to our modest effort to work things out. We know that the evil does not entirely fill up our world. It can be seen as set in something larger that we have frequently approved. It does not represent God completely. He has other things to say and do, even in this dark happening that is molesting us now.

Whilst a well-organized spiritual life will be enthusiastic about its enjoyments, there obviously has to be some attempt at simplification. You can't keep too many things on your mind and be happy. So work out what freight you are going to carry in that container and don't exceed; it is not all that robust. Too much joy is no different in this issue from too much pain. What throws you is the one more, whatever it is.

You have to select. You can't make use of even half of what

interests you. Settle for what you have found most deeply stirs your being, stays good in the memory, is worth being found dead with. That must be the way of life. You are not alive until you know who you are and what you are looking for; and there is no route to that other than through 'the labyrinth of choice' – I will have this, not that.

Whatever I am, it must have something to do with what I most often choose, though perhaps that is not what the deepest voice in me is asking for, and everyone needs help just there. All sane people, religious or not, want to live a true life, that is to say, a life that is their own, an individual thing, not a sell-out to society or convention, and one that is in harmony with the truth about themselves.

And the truth about every human being, or part of it, is that there are experiences he can take and make use of, and there are experiences that are too much for him; he cannot absorb them, he is damaged by them or held up in some way. A healthy respect for that is useful.

It is not true that it does not matter what happens to us, that whatever happens is all experience and experience as such is worth having. That is an exaggeration, and exaggeration is often exciting, but someone must stand by the truth.

There are obviously many experiences that are not worth having at all, like being intensely cruel, like hating someone so much you dream of it. And there are many experiences it is better not to have too soon; for example, no one would want a child to have an experience of absolute terror or the icy sense of being some kind of outcast.

So one has to select not only the quantity but the quality of one's experiences. The occasional nervous, uneasy prayer about this is nothing to be ashamed of. Jesus included something of that kind, here, in the prayer he taught his friends.

One of the most attractive and slippery ideas that Christianity has set before the world is a kind of de-moralizing of love. Right action, doing the will of God, coming through the encounter with evil, is to be seen as done by man and God together. It is a form of loving. Rightness, righteousness is the bloom on loving.

In the tenth book of his *Confessions* St Augustine, from the immense despair stretched between his heart and the good he does not really want to do, sees light at last in the merciful arrangement by which God himself gives to the loving Christian the specific obedience he is asking from him. If that is the situation, it means, at any rate theoretically, that life is saved from moral strain. Whatever we ought to do is not done by the strenuous summoning of our sense of duty but is in fact given us to do by God as a natural result of our loving him. It flows out of that love.

So St Augustine says 'All my hope is nowhere but in thy exceeding great mercy. Give what thou commandest and command what thou wilt.'

Let God ask anything he likes from us as long as he gives us the spiritual wherewithal to do it.

The famous idea 'love God and do what you like' is an epigrammatic summary of this bit of Augustinian wisdom. It needs to be seen in its context. Its depth of truth is not always registered by bright-eyed lovers who use it as a romantic rebel's flag to carry in a stuffy world.

To understand right behaviour as loving is certainly one of the special goods Christianity has to offer, though it is not always in the shop-window, where there is often a pile of uninteresting moral verbiage. Most people realize that you could in fact obey most moral rules yet loving could nevertheless by no means be your strong suit, that is to say, loving as a free movement of your whole self, imaginative, widely-responsive, inventive.

Today there is a vast literature of protest against traditional ideas of goodness; and, incidentally, in much of it you can hear if not the voice then echoes of the voice of the man of Nazareth. He does seem to be the spiritual source of the best thoughts the world has had on all this, which must be why he still holds that solitary place to which so many people go back, as if they suspected it is there and only there that some sense of rightness could come into one's life.

Anyone trying to fathom the sayings of Jesus, and comparing his own fear of evil with the dread in Jesus' mind, begins to have new ideas about what it is that really threatens us all. There is much to be said for interpreting the great temptation now, however it was specifically understood at first, in terms of what clearly alarmed Jesus most. And that was, without doubt, a mind closed, for whatever reason, to the coming of God, to the coming of love.

There is only one temptation really. It is the temptation against love, to refuse it when it is offered to you, to deny its presence within you when it is there, to act as though you no longer believe in it, to follow other lights. These rejections of love are what we now see evil to be.

The twentieth century is so full of temptations to people to use up their precious emotions in what is less than loving or against it that a cynic could be forgiven for thinking of love as the flower beneath the world's foot. I mean our time's assiduous cultivation of cheap love, stupid love, portentous love (as seen in many moralists and anti-moralists). Then there is the egoistic thing – as of lovers contemplating their own reflections in the pool of each other's mind, so absorbed in this mutual image that no one else and nothing else is of interest. The mark is missed possibly most often in sentimental love – 'the sentimentalist is he who would enjoy without incurring the immense debtorship for a thing done'.[4] The list could be prolonged; but long or short it includes of course the temptation to note such failures and evasions and casualties of loving as though one has somehow escaped oneself and has no need of what mercy is available.

God's will is always some form of loving. The evil that is in our power to do or to resist is consequently some kind of withdrawal from the world of love, an avoiding of the risk and effort of loving, or a stopping-short of the real thing and settling for a cheap imitation of it.

The question is, what is the real thing? The Christian answer is that that is exactly what we are put into this world to learn, and that the wisdom of Jesus is the light by which we can most interestingly learn it.

However much or little of this learning we have done, all of us are faced with one situation after another in which what we see to be sensible and productive of life, or just the next useful step in some ordinary human tangle, is going to involve us in some effort (perhaps just to see another's point of view) or some disadvantage to ourselves or a period of loneliness. It is then we are inclined to pull back.

On this view, temptation is not some seduction, whispering beguilingly, as in many a Victorian hymn's theatrical description of sin, but an avoidance of the effort of loving, or being unwilling to risk the pain involved, or being so angry about something that one just cannot shift the inner load of aggression and be free to love.

To be unwilling to make the efforts of imagination that are involved in loving is often due to the fear that a fuller appreciation of the situation will mean change in oneself, at least the surrendering of some partial view that has served a useful purpose up to now, either as stoking the fires of resentment or convincing one that nothing can be done to improve matters.

The risk involved in loving is often the same thing, the risk of change. Our affections and demands, our expectations and dislikes, and all the rest that goes to make what we are, form a structure, firm here, shaky there, quite useless there; but, for better and worse, that is the me I carry around. Because in places this structure is ill-fitting and shaky, it very easily feels threatened. To ask if one's anger in some issue is really necessary is a challenge to what one is, and so it can be seen as a threat, even though it may actually mean putting one's foot on the first rung of the ladder of a new happiness.

It seems that much of our struggle with life's evil is in some such way primarily a struggle with ourselves. Every mature religion that has brightened the life of man has urged on him the wisdom of looking within, of considering his customary attitudes and reactions, and estimating their appropriateness or their poison.

If it is true that the only evil we should fear is that of losing the power to love, or stifling it, when only love can save anything from the turmoil of life, we shall want to make use of this wisdom.

So, Jesus, made use of the inwardness of his own tradition, and with such understanding that he has become our chosen teacher of it. It comes to us now so clearly in his voice, his persuasive way of speaking directly to the mind and the feelings at once, that if we left him who else could take his place as life's redemption?

The point of looking within is not to withdraw from practical life but to see the world outside oneself more clearly. We tend to interpret our encounters with others (persons, facts, problems) in terms of our own wants and fears, and so we cannot help sometimes seeing what is not there. Unless we look within and catch sight of this wishful-thinking process that is continually going on, we shall never guess its power. We all have to use what wits we have, and for some this means what wits we have left after one or other of life's better-aimed blows. Things do not exist just for the glow they may generate in your life. Life has to do with people and affairs 'out there'. It is not just a convenient arrangement of mirrors. The force of this simple truth (truism is the better word) never strikes one until one looks within and sees oneself forgetting it.

It is part of the same condition that when things 'out there' go wrong we find it hard to think that the failures of other people could possibly be attributed to any insufficiency in us to meet their legitimate needs and expectations. If anyone is to blame it is always someone else.

Much in our culture supports and strengthens this blindness. The literature of crime and detection, the science-fiction novel and film, while a valid part of our fantasy life, are popular also because they externalize wrongness and accustom us to thinking of it as a threat from without instead of from within. They comfort us by simplifying our perplexity about the mystery of evil (its personal, national, international dimensions), by presenting someone else as the great wrong-doer, clearly defined and as far from us as possible – an agent from outer space, a product of a laboratory – whom competent forces will track down.

Not loving is the great evil, because human beings function best when loving, always deteriorate without it, and because there is so much to love: from human beings, the natural world, the sun's greatness reducing to a last red rim before darkness, the sea endlessly emptying itself on the shore and endlessly finding more to give, music and the way each repeated hearing gains from the ones preceding it and adds pressure of meaning to those to come, all the living mystery and need of what is damaged and perverted, to all life's immensely relieving, ridiculous side – starlings, ducks, the Synod. The list is endless; and so it should be, because a spiritual being develops through likings and the more you clutter up yourself with dislikings the more you fade into nonentity.

Not loving is the disaster most to be feared. You have to remind yourself of that, your credo, again and again, and set yourself to recover it when you lose hold of it. In the worship of the church we could do with rather better help than most of the crumby hymns of praise we have to sing. And if the Litany, with its monumental gravity and gloom, is a necessary spiritual exercise, it should have a companion piece, perhaps in similar form to stress the point, full of summary affirmations of human delight and affection.

Even so, there are all the secondary evils, the losses and failures, which come in infinite variety to all but are always experienced singly, as the pressure of particular pain on some unhappy individual who can or cannot bear it.

It is a pity if one always has to organize from scratch an adequate response to cope with misfortune. There certainly has to be some specific mobilization of oneself, but it is good if people can acquire some continuing readiness and sophistication with which they actually meet trouble and so defuse some of it on contact.

Much of life goes wrong for everyone; some of it is sure to go wrong for me. I shall negotiate trouble more successfully if I abandon the common but usually unconscious assumption that things ought to go right, that it is unfair that there should be friction or failure in my own life. If I can work that into my day-to-day stance, when things do go wrong I shall be free from the wastage of energy involved in being immediately furious and depressed, and be able to have a reasonable shot at thinking out what can be done.

On the other hand, there is a limit to useful preparation. It is a common human experience that what people think beforehand they cannot possibly do or bear they often find they actually can do or bear when the time comes, if they are willing to receive what is given them in that hour. Young people, particularly, often dread more than can ever happen to them.

There is a grace in things, even darkest things, to which we need to keep open. When you are feeling down and you go to the eucharist, even though negative prayers are supposed to be unintelligent, it is good to ask for grace not to resist the grace that is there, to be as relaxed as possible and ready to accept the invisible, impalpable help that is certainly being given. Which is, like all sacramental moments, a representative image of the real presence in every moment.

When we have done what we can, some improvement may be clear, but not all will be set right; there will also be some failure, some remaining difficulties. We have to make the best of this residuum. In it there is always some good, there is the grace of what good it can bear. It is the grace of God.

Incidentally, your idea of God is usually the mirror-image of your idea of life. If you are not fair to life you will weight the scales against God. There are people who see what is wrong far more clearly than what is right and soon are hardly seeing what is right at all. They are of the opinion that the face of life is perfectly designed to express tragedy. That fatuous view fails to recognize that even what is wrong is not always tragic or outrageous or inexplicable. Even very severe anguish is often not a problem for the rational mind.

Much mental and spiritual suffering, which is sometimes

quite terrifying, is a sign of a whole person struggling to survive, to adapt and grow and come out into the light again.

Baudelaire spoke of suffering as the great fertilizer of spiritual life, and he had particularly excruciating experience of it. Think of some of the suffering of adolescence, of the strains and tensions of early marriage, of the new range of anxiety quietly creeping up on people from the back of their minds when they enter the second half of life, of how it always takes more of yourself than you imagined would be needed to cope with disappointment, with success, with grief.

All are instances of the self seeking a new adaptation, a new set of values, revising its understanding of what really matters, finding out where to go from here. None of it can be done without pain, because whenever a person reaches one of these critical points of growth, the perplexed self splits, and half wants to go on and half wants to hang back.

But it is not negative or useless pain. It is really grace, the presence, the coming of the kingdom; and you could in time be thankful for it and want to include it in what you mean when you say 'and let all that is within me praise his holy name'.

Many people believe in God but are not sure now that the celestial system they learned about as children is any good. Their prayers return to them like rejected coins from a public telephone that no longer works. It does work, but it is not constructed for that shape of coin. What you have to put in is not requests for favours but longings to understand. 'Lord I believe; help thou my unbelief' is the right size. And the little that you in fact believe and want helped, want deepened, since it officially goes back to Jesus, often needs to be checked by what he said and what he made of life.

He was in no doubt whatever about the place of pain in the world's fulfilment, though right from the start he had difficulty in persuading others to take his view. In the New Testament the disciples are presented to us as representative of those interesting, restless people who for one reason or another up-root themselves and go in search of another world – in their case along with this man who had the charisma that does not often gather round anyone, confidence in life. They felt that his presence would light the way to a world far more interesting than any they could make or find for themselves. It was with some dismay that they found that over him hung an extra-ordinary sense of death.

It was not at all the sense of death with which we are familiar, a veil of sadness and fear that hangs between twentieth-century people and any good meaning that death could possibly have. It was death accepted, and accepted without question.

Jesus was not provoked into our anxieties and speculations by the knowledge that eventually you have to leave your last friend behind and go on alone. He thought of it as part of God's providence, just as much as life is, and in itself not to be feared. Mortality was entirely dwarfed by the sense of God's presence, whatever we are doing or suffering or enjoying, and his con-viction about the joy that is prepared for us beyond tomorrow.

Even so, there is a world of difference between an abstraction like mortality and the death each person dies or will die. His had a special dread for Jesus in that, having no illusions about his own situation and the manner of death he would die, the thought of death gave a sinister intensity and cost to all he attempted to do for God.

It is still correct to say that he did not fear death in itself as we tend to do. He had a different view of it, as indeed of almost everything human beings can fear. If love is what matters most, God's love and our loving, it is right to follow him in seeing death as set in that infinitely bigger thing. It is part of God's love for us that we are alive. It is part of his love that we die. That we should suffer the preliminary, lesser deaths that are our losses and failures is also part of his love, as his speaking to us through them of life's continual movement and all the loss and gain of growth.

Henry James would not be considered Christian in any formal sense, but he was in at the deep end of this truth when, in a letter to a friend grieving over the death of Rupert Brooke, among the tenderest condolences he wrote:

> All my impulse is to tell you to entertain the pang and taste the bitterness for all they are 'worth' – to know to the fullest extent what has happened to you and not miss one of the hard ways in which it will come home.[5]

To see in some such way that the pang and bitterness of painful experience are not negative, not simply the violence of life and the heart's impoverishment under it, but that something precious is given in them that reaches us in no other way, so that it would be wisdom to go through with them, feeling them 'for all they are worth' – that is to be not far from the kingdom of God.

We would less frequently misconstrue testing experiences as evils if it were not for the nuisance of self-preoccupation. Much of what we fear is made up of agitation about what has happened or what may yet happen to ourselves.

People who are most alive seem to be able to resist this restricted viewpoint and to keep in touch with experience in the large, the world's extraordinary tangle of millions of lives and deaths, and all the goodness and beauty drifting about in it waiting to be loved.

It is this imaginative spread of their lives into as much interest and enjoyment as possible that reduces self-preoccupation, simply by bringing them more pleasure. The less there is in one's life, the larger looms one's self. The larger it looms, the more dissatisfied it seems to be.

The positive relation between pleasure and the sense of salvation (the sense of being a whole self, not distracted by grievance and apprehension) has never been given its due in traditional spirituality. It has been wrongly confused with selfishness, whereas actually it is a going forward into an enlarging world of appreciations and a release from the circumscribed ego.

An adult response to life will still, along with this warm approach, be keenly aware of the intractability of things. There are problems that are never solved; there are genuine improvements that simultaneously seem to take back what they give by exposing areas of need that were not even suspected in the unremedied condition. Some of the tangles in which life is snarled for both young and old can be smoothed out only if a score of forces, individual and social, are mobilized here and there and even far away.

Some evils are indeed overcome, it is true, not always obviously, because many factors are involved in any progress we make. These factors include our own efforts, helps of many kinds, both sought and unexpected, enthusiasm shed into the difficult area from other parts of one's life that are going well, the untraceable use God makes of the prayers and affection of others, even simply the passage of time. Much of this is unseen. It is to the backward look, to the recalling of past time (which is the bread and wine of faith) that one's own journey surprisingly takes its place in life's general worth and dignity and is caught up into all our long grief and gratitude for Christ.

In most people of average generosity today is to be found the mixture of compassion and interest and question which is as near as our generation comes to having an ideal. It is a reasonable and indeed admirable mixture.

Compassion is surely the normal response of people, who still have some light in their eyes and some movement in their hearts, to the sight of so much opportunity and difficulty, so much delight and outrage, which this world presents.

Interest is just about the primary sign of health – interest in what is going on, interest in what is missing and therefore required in the current situation, interest in becoming and being oneself (Jesus thought that to fail in the latter could not be compensated for by the entire world).

The questioning is just inevitable. It follows the compassion and the interest. They take the mind into the need and the beauty of the world, where all the questions are, irresistibly waiting to be asked. The need and the beauty of the world cannot bring the mind to rest. You cannot rest in the thought that life is simply a great brotherhood of compassion, a fellowship of suffering, even though it is not an ignoble thought. And the beauty of the world, because, to use Keats' words, it has always made human beings feel existence supremely, has necessarily for that reason shown how quiet death is. And off goes the mind on the longest, mistiest journey. The longest journey is the search for meaning, for what it is that life seems to be saying and the even more important thing it promises yet to say.

Life has no meaning in the usual sense of the word, in the sense that a word has a meaning that we can look up in a dictionary, or a sentence has a meaning whose ideas can be expressed perhaps more clearly in other words. 'How I distrust neat designs of life that are drawn upon half-sheets of note-paper.' So Virginia Woolf, and she goes on to prefer some design 'more in accordance with those moments of humiliation and triumph that come now and then undeniably'.[6]

However, a great, sprawling, complicated religion like Christianity is a different affair. It is not a half-sheet of notepaper. When people say that life has meaning because of Christian faith, they are referring to Christian faith as a way of thinking about human experiences, and living through them, that holds them together in a pattern that is acceptable to the mind, is not inconsistent with any known fact, normally maintains life's interest and hopefulness, and revives these when stress or distress reduces or temporarily destroys them.

Such a faith gathers conviction the more it is used, because it is found to do justice to more and more areas of life as we become acquainted with them. So it naturally tends to have more 'meaning' for people as they grow older and have in their memories many encounters with perplexity and disaster, with the inexplicably beautiful, and with their own vulnerability. All these, and much else, are seen or felt to have a relatedness, to be in an all-enfolding sympathy.

Consequently, the great religious images and symbols and metaphors accumulate a great weight of significance, and can sometimes make many others resonate in the mind. The eucharist has this packed presence for a great many people. For others, certain hymns, if sung lingeringly and sagely enough, the voices firmly together in the sense of song and the embrace of faith, can bring them to the brink of tears, since they too sound as a reminiscence, an *anamnesis*, exposing the infinite depth of our tradition all the way back to Jesus' bitter intimacy with death and the bright mystery of another kind of life that he brought us.

In the 'Our Father' we have the best possible recall to his mind, to his understanding of what God means by our being here. Coming as it did from his own lips it must on ours give us confidence that in intention we are standing where he stood.

Kierkegaard said of praying 'in the name of Jesus' that it means to pray 'in such a manner that I dare name Jesus in it, that is to say, think of him, think his holy will together with whatever I am praying for'. That is not always easy. You think you are thinking of him when really what is in your mind is some variant that your own memories and desires have fabricated. It could disguise rather than recall him; which is what the Bible must mean by honouring God with your lips while your heart is far from him. Some of that must always be going on, the elusive heart being not so much under our control as our thundering preachers seem to have imagined. His prayer is worth trusting to keep that within bounds.

In calling God 'Our Father' in his characteristically affectionate way he is understood to mean that our life is the means by which we learn about loving, about God loving us, and our loving God and in him all other human beings and life itself. Loving God is done mainly by faith. Indeed loving anyone has to have a lot of faith in it because there is so much in loving that is dark and unmapped.

In loving God, the faith is to believe that the whole structure of things (both what you can see and what is going on invisibly all the time) is itself one multitudinous process of love. Its purpose is to provide the conditions under which we can best develop and express such ability to love as temporal limitations allow. It is the best of all possible worlds for this, though not a very good one for any other dominant purpose.

Everyone really wants to love without limit. Most of the mess the world is in is due to this huge want getting out of hand or being misunderstood. That is not to be wondered at, because obviously a world of limited loves is going to be a trouble to and make trouble for this limitless want.

So we believe that the learning of love must continue after

death, in new contexts and dimensions and appropriate opportunities, until it is completed. And anyone who wants that explained must know that it is impossible, because it lies outside human life and language, and anything we say about it soon sounds ridiculous.

Yet it is what Jesus believed in, passionately longed for, and taught his friends to pray for.

Every attempt at loving is in itself both a preparation for and a reflection of that fulfilment of loving that God intends for his creation.

All reverences and admirations, even misguided ones, every good purpose that shares life's bread and makes a family of mankind, all forgivenesses and other new beginnings and recoveries of freedom, all testings of this faith that show it holding through good and ill, all these have a sacramental character in that in them the eternal end for which human beings were created to some extent *comes*. It comes forward, presses into time, to whet time's appetite, to give mankind a glimpse of what it is all for, of what is rightly admired and delighted in, what eventually will be the only and absolutely real.

Jesus is the supreme example of this loving in which the 'end' of the world comes and is seen.

We order our loving and living by the light that is in him.

He stands as the promise of the life that will be ours beyond tomorrow.

NOTES

Our Father who art in heaven

1. Edwin Muir, *Collected Poems*, Faber 1960, p. 227.
2. *Methodist Hymn Book*, 339; cf. Gen. 32.13–32.

Hallowed by thy name

1. Paul Scott, *The Chinese Love Pavilion*, Heinemann 1967; Panther Books 1973, p. 63.
2. Martin Buber, *Between Man and Man*, Kegan Paul 1947, p. 43.
3. Martin Buber, *Mamre,* Melbourne University Press 1946, p. 20.
4. Martin Buber, *Eclipse of God*, Harper & Row, NY 1957, pp. 7f.

Thy kingdom come

1. Raymond Chandler, *Pearls are a Nuisance*, Penguin 1969, pp. 7f.
2. Graham Greene, *A Sort of Life*, The Bodley Head 1971; Penguin 1974, p. 121.

Give us this day our daily bread

1. Joachim Jeremias, *The Prayers of Jesus*, SCM Press 1967, pp. 99–102; see also, G. Wainwright, *Eucharist and Eschatology*, Epworth Press 1971, pp. 30–34.
2. Sister Edna Mary, *The Religious Life*, Penguin 1968, pp. 116ff; see also, F. J. Moloney, *Free to Love*, Darton Longman & Todd 1981.

And forgive us our debts

1. Joachim Jeremias, *The Prayers of Jesus*, SCM Press 1967, p. 92.
2. C. H. Dodd, *The Founder of Christianity*, Collins 1971, pp. 96f.
3. G. W. Russell, *Collected Poems*, Macmillan 1935.

And lead us not into temptation

1. Franz Kafka, *The Castle*, Secker & Warburg 1971; Penguin 1975.
2. Thomas Merton, *The Wisdom of the Desert*, Sheldon Press 1974, p. 56.
3. See Joachim Jeremias, *The Prayers of Jesus*, SCM Press 1967, p. 105.
4. James Joyce, *Ulysses*, The Bodley Head 1960; Penguin 1969, p. 199.
5. *The Letters of Henry James*, ed. P. Lubbock, 1920, vol. 2, p. 486.
6. Virginia Woolf, *The Waves*, The Hogarth Press 1943; Penguin 1969, p. 204.